IMAGES
of Aviation

WRIGHT FIELD

The Wright Field spearhead insignia is attributed to Maj. Hugh Kneer (later Gen. Hugh Kneer) and was authorized for use no later than January 1931. The design symbolically points the way forward. Appearing in two sizes, it also served as the insignia for all Air Depot aircraft, with the depot's initials displayed inside (FAD for Fairfield Air Depot, SAD for Sacramento Air Depot, and so forth). In 1942, Technical Order 01-1-21 replaced it with the gear and propeller emblem of the Air Service Command, though the Middletown and San Antonio Air Depots continued using it as late as December 1953. (Author's collection.)

ON THE COVER: German, British, and American aircraft are displayed during the Army Air Forces (AAF) Air Fair held in October 1945. The largest air show ever held at Wright Field, the 1945 AAF Air Fair celebrated the end of World War II with displays of American, British, and captured enemy warplanes, many seen for the first time. The weeklong event attracted nearly one million visitors from 27 countries. (See page 114.) (National Museum of the United States Air Force.)

IMAGES
of Aviation

WRIGHT FIELD

Kenneth M. Keisel

ARCADIA
PUBLISHING

Published by Arcadia Publishing
Charleston, South Carolina

Printed in the United States of America

Library of Congress Control Number: 2015955092

For all general information, please contact Arcadia Publishing:
Telephone 843-853-2070
Fax 843-853-0044
E-mail sales@arcadiapublishing.com
For customer service and orders:
Toll-Free 1-888-313-2665

Visit us on the Internet at www.arcadiapublishing.com

The empty room shown here was located in the newly completed Wright Field Administration Building (Building 11). In 1927, it became home to the Wright Field Photographic Unit. Many of the photographs in this book were developed and printed in this room by men and women serving in the US Army Signal Corps Photographic Units. It is to these men and women that this book is dedicated. They served their country in rooms like this in countless locations around the globe. During times of war and peace, they spent endless hours photographing, developing, and printing images that may have seemed insignificant at the time, but are now priceless records of America's military history. Without their dedication and service, books like this simply would not be possible. (National Museum of the United States Air Force.)

CONTENTS

ACKNOWLEDGMENTS

The creation of this book would not have been possible without the generous assistance of a great many people who were just as dedicated to telling the story of Wright Field as I. Many thanks go to Dr. Henry Narducci of the Air Force Life Cycle Management Center History Office. Whole sections of this book would have been impossible without his assistance. Thanks also go to Brett A. Stolle, photo archivist for the National Museum of the United States Air Force, and to Paul Woodruff, historian for the Air Force Material Command, who is himself writing a book on Wright Field that I encourage readers to purchase. In addition, I wish to thank Andrew Glasgow and the entire Glasgow family for the photographs and information they provided related to Capt. William C. Glasgow's tragic crash in May 1945. I also want to thank Julian Halliday for once again giving new life to old photographs. Thanks go to Jesse Darland and Jeff Ruetsche at Arcadia Publishing for continuing to see the importance in telling the story of these great American air bases. Finally, I wish to thank the many engineers, authors, and archivists whose work provided invaluable references for the text of this book, including, but not limited to, Diana G. Cornelisse, Mary Ann Johnson, Kenneth Chilstrom, and William F. Bahret.

In order to keep text to a minimum, photographs provided by the Air Force Life Cycle Management Center History Office are credited as "AFLCMC," while those from the National Museum of the United States Air Force are credited as "NMUSAF."

Unless otherwise noted, all aircraft photographs in this book were taken at Wright Field. No stock photographs were used in the making of this book.

INTRODUCTION

"Dream your boldest dreams, multiply by 10, and you will fall short," was marshal of France Joseph Joffre's reply when, in the spring of 1917, American military leaders asked him how large we should make America's air force. Following years of apathy, America had allowed its allies and enemies to surpass it both in aircraft design and in numbers. When the time came for the United States to enter World War I, America was forced to turn to its allies for aircraft capable of defeating Germany. Dayton, Ohio, home to the Wright brothers and the birthplace of aviation, would once again become the center of American aviation research and development. In 1917, McCook Field, located just north of downtown, became home to the Army's Airplane Engineering Department. Soon, Dayton residents could watch as the world's greatest aircraft soared across the skies over their city. Meanwhile, just a few miles south in Moraine, Ohio, the Dayton-Wright Aircraft Company was producing up to 40 de Havilland DH-4 airplanes a day for the war effort. The residents of Dayton were going to make sure that America never again fell short in the field of military air power. This became Dayton's mission—started in 1903 by Wilbur and Orville Wright, expanded in 1917 by the establishment of McCook Field, and fulfilled in 1927 with the creation of Wright Field. It is a mission that continues today at Wright-Patterson Air Force Base.

This book examines the role that Wright Field played in that mission, from its founding in 1927 until the establishment of Wright-Patterson Air Force Base in 1948. It continues a story begun in my previous book *Dayton Aviation: The Wright Brothers to McCook Field*. In this book, you will find scores of amazing photographs that reveal the vital role Wright Field played between the wars by keeping the US Army Air Corps a world leader in aircraft design and development. World War II catapulted Wright Field into the forefront of America's war effort, as virtually every new aircraft developed for the US Army Air Corps was tested and evaluated in Dayton. Wright Field's testing program also had the fascinating task of studying captured enemy aircraft, some powered by jet engines, which engineers at Wright Field were also developing. This book also examines the base's impact on the local community by providing thousands of jobs as well as some of the greatest air shows ever held in the United States. Finally, a collection of crash photographs reveals the often tragic consequences that inevitably come with the testing of advanced experimental aircraft.

It is my hope that all Dayton residents will learn to appreciate the connection between their city and the history of aviation—not just as aviation's birthplace but also the ongoing role Dayton has played in the development of military and civilian aviation over the last century. The skies over Dayton are truly "Hallowed Skies." Were it possible to place a historical marker at every point in Dayton's sky where a historic flight had occurred, they would cast a shadow over the entire city. Since we cannot do that, the photographs in this book must suffice; and if they do not take the Douglas XB-19 bomber and place it in your living room or bring the 1945 AAF Air Show into your den, I hope they do something very much like it.

Throughout its history, the various areas of Wright Field have had a dizzying array of names—so many that aviation historians often struggle with using the correct title when referring to a specific event. If we are confused, we understand completely if you are too. It is beyond the scope of this book to explain all the many names employed at Wright Field over the years, but here is a brief explanation that I hope will help reduce the confusion.

Wright Field can trace its ancestry back to two military bases that once occupied the site. The first was Wilbur Wright Field, a World War I US Army Signal Corps pilot training field, which opened on June 6, 1917. The second was the Fairfield Aviation General Supply Depot, a triangular-shaped, 40-acre storage and supply facility, which opened on January 4, 1918. Both were located within Area C, which, as of 2012, is now part of Area A. (See what I mean?) To make matters worse, the Fairfield Aviation General Supply Depot underwent five name changes before closing on January 1, 1946.

On August 21, 1925, the name Wilbur Wright Field was officially struck by the War Department. On that day, all 4,324 acres of land donated by the citizens of Dayton were officially renamed Wright Field.

Wright Field was actually comprised of two separate bases with two distinctly different missions. The area east of the Huffman Dam (Area C) was primarily for supply and logistics, while a new area located west of the dam (Area B) was for aircraft research and development. This new area opened its doors on October 12, 1927. Though the name Wright Field initially applied to the entire base, by the early 1930s, it referred primarily to the area located west of the Huffman Dam (Area B).

On July 1, 1931, a 2,075-acre area, which included the former Wilbur Wright Field, was renamed Patterson Field. In 1944, it was also given the designation Area C. Though Patterson Field fell under a different command than Wright Field, it was initially considered a portion of Wright Field, as that name applied to the entire base. On January 13, 1948, Wright Field and Patterson Field were merged to form Wright-Patterson Air Force Base.

The names Area A, Area B, and Area C were created on August 21, 1944, when it was decided that the functions of Wright Field and Patterson Field would be better served under a single command. The creation of Areas B and C was straightforward, but Area A's was somewhat comical. Though Patterson Field fell under the command of Wright Field, the physical location for the headquarters was to be Patterson Field. This upset Wright Field's commanding officers, who did not want Wright Field's headquarters inside Patterson Field. To solve the problem, a portion of Patterson Field containing the new headquarters was renamed Area A and transferred to Wright Field. The area of Wright Field located west of the Huffman Dam was renamed Area B, while the remainder of Patterson Field and the Fairfield Aviation General Supply Depot were renamed Area C. In 2012, Areas A and C were finally reunited, and the name Area C was dropped. For several years, the name Area D was applied to Skyway Park, a 119-acre base housing community, which closed in 1963 and is now part of Wright State University. Because many readers will be more familiar with the Area A-B-C designations, these will be included in the text whenever possible, though it is important to remember that they were not implemented until 1944.

ABOUT THE MATERIEL DIVISION

The history of McCook Field, Wright Field, and Wright-Patterson Air Force Base is forever tied to the history of the Materiel Division (now Air Force Materiel Command). From its founding at McCook Field in 1917, the purpose of the Materiel Division was to develop, test, and acquire every piece of equipment needed by the Army Air Service. This included everything from bombs to lifeboats, from parachutes to flight jackets, and everything in between, including all the aircraft used by the Air Service. In the case of aircraft acquisition, the process underwent four distinct changes, leading up to the method employed by the US Air Force today.

When the United States entered World War I in 1917, the Army Air Service was shocked to learn that its aircraft were completely outdated compared to those of Germany, France, England, and Italy. It attributed this to an American aircraft industry that had failed to keep up with its counterparts in Europe. The Air Service believed the solution was to design, test, and manufacture its own aircraft. Purchases from civilian manufacturers would be eliminated whenever possible. The Army even established an Air Service Engineering School at McCook Field to produce personnel capable of designing and manufacturing new aircraft. From the day it opened in 1917, McCook Field was intended to be a facility for both aircraft design and manufacturing.

By the mid-1920s, it was apparent that the Air Service's plan to manufacture its own aircraft was pushing its resources to their limits, as well as hindering the growth of America's civilian aircraft industry. By the time the Materiel Division relocated to Wright Field in 1927, the Air Service was no longer designing and manufacturing its own aircraft. Wright Field's mission changed to the development, testing, and acquisition of new aircraft purchased from civilian manufacturers. In order to determine the best aircraft design, competitions would be held to test prototypes, with the winner receiving a production contract.

The competition process worked well throughout the 1930s and resulted in many of the legendary aircraft used in World War II, but by the early 1940s, it was apparent that the production of costly prototypes drained precious resources needed for the war effort. Instead, new aircraft were often selected and put into production straight off the drawing board. During World War II, the purpose of Wright Field changed to the testing and refinement of preproduction models.

As the war wound down, it became clear that producing aircraft straight off the drawing board resulted in too many issues that had to be resolved during production. By the time the US Air Force was established in 1947, Wright Field was once again holding competitions between competing "Y" planes. Since competitions resumed at Wright Field in the mid-1940s, they have become the Air Force's preferred method of selecting new combat aircraft. In 1991, following flight tests, the Lockheed Martin F-22 Raptor was selected over Northrop's F-23 Black Widow II. In 2001, the Lockheed Martin F-35 Lightning II defeated the Boeing X-32, and in 2015, Lockheed-Boeing and Nothrop-Grumman battled for the coveted Long Range Strike Bomber contract. Though flight-testing had moved in the late 1940s to Edwards Air Force Base, the staff of Air Force Materiel Command, based at Wright-Patterson Air Force Base, still plays a crucial role in determining the winning aircraft.

One

1917–1929
FROM MCCOOK FIELD TO WRIGHT FIELD

Dayton has experience two close calls—moments when it looked like Dayton would forever lose its place on aviation's world stage. The first was in 1917, the year the Wright Company, which Wilbur and Orville had established on West Third Street, closed its doors and moved out of town. Orville sold the business in 1915 to a group of investors who quickly determined there was no benefit in keeping it in Dayton. Aviation, it seemed, was leaving Dayton behind.

In stepped Col. Edward A. Deeds, the former president of National Cash Register (NCR). Deeds had powerful connections in the US Army and was able to accomplish two goals. First, he organized a new aircraft company in Moraine, Ohio. The Dayton-Wright Aircraft Company was soon producing up to 40 de Havilland DH-4 biplanes a day for the war in Europe. Second, Deeds helped establish McCook Field. Located at a bend in the Great Miami River just north of downtown, McCook Field played a vital role from 1917 until 1927 as the test facility for all new aircraft entering US Army Air Corps service.

The second close call came in 1922, when the Army made known its intentions to close McCook Field. A newer, larger, and more advanced research facility was needed to test the powerful new aircraft coming into Army Air Corps service. The Army was looking at locations in Michigan and Virginia to house this base. For the second time in just five years, it looked like aviation was leaving Dayton behind, but the residents of Dayton would never let that happen.

The origin of Wright Field can be traced back to a single individual, Dayton industrialist Edward A. Deeds. Deeds served as president of National Cash Register (NCR), as well as president of the Miami Conservancy District, which gave him control over thousands of acres of land along the Great Miami River floodplain. In 1917, Deeds learned from his connections in Washington, DC, that the US Army was having difficulty with a joint Army and Navy aircraft research facility being built in Langley, Virginia. Construction of the base was running behind schedule and over budget, and it appeared likely that it would not be completed before the United States entered World War I. Deeds offered to lease the Army an area of land he owned just north of downtown Dayton as a temporary site for the facility. The Army accepted Deeds's offer, and in 1917, McCook Field was constructed. From 1917 until 1927, McCook Field served as the site for all US Army aircraft research and development. (AFLCMC.)

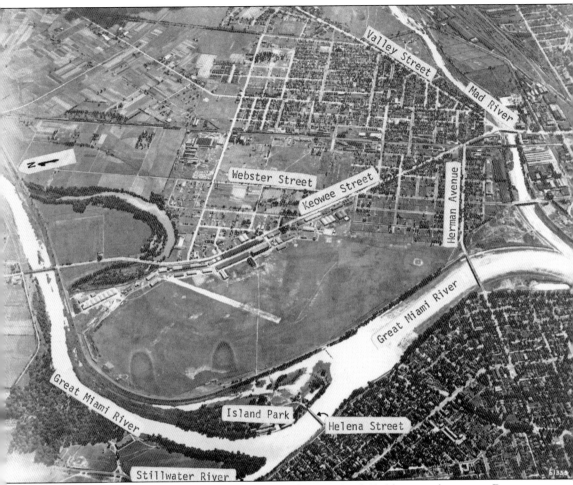

Taken around 1921, this photograph shows how close McCook Field was to downtown Dayton. From 1917 until 1927, Dayton office workers could look out their windows and watch history being made in the skies over their city. As McCook Field was home to the Army's aircraft Engineering Division, an extensive list of aviation "firsts" took place there, including the first flight in a pressurized aircraft, the first crop dusting flight, and the first flight using radio beacon guidance, as well as one altitude record after another. The field was laid out by Orville Wright. Prevailing winds forced the construction of the runway across its narrowest point. Airplanes that overshot the runway would end up in the Great Miami River, and many did. The runway was only 1,000 feet long and 100 feet wide, sufficient for aircraft of 1917. But as airplanes grew more powerful, this would soon change. (AFLCMC.)

The early 1920s saw the arrival of the Army's first heavy bomber, the massive Barling Bomber. When it first flew on August 22, 1923, the Barling Bomber was the world's largest airplane. McCook Field's runway was too short for the Barling Bomber, so it had to be hangared and flown from Wilbur Wright Field, 10 miles away. The enormous Barling Bomber was the first of many heavy bombers to be tested in Dayton. (AFLCMC.)

"This field is small—use it all" was McCook Field's motto, as displayed in this photograph taken in the mid-1920s. By 1920, the situation at McCook was escalating. As more and more powerful airplanes were developed, the field's size became an increasing problem. On March 1, 1918, the staff at McCook requested permission to use Wilbur Wright Field, located 10 miles away, for some experimental flying. By the time McCook Field closed in 1927, virtually all flight tests had moved to Wilbur Wright Field. (AFLCMC.)

By the early 1920s, the situation at McCook Field had grown desperate. Encroaching residential development prevented base expansion, and the field's proximity to downtown made leasing the property expensive. In 1922, the Army announced that it would close McCook Field. To make matters worse, a group in Michigan had offered the Army free land if it relocated there, eliminating the need for congressional approval. For Ed Deeds, the timing could not have been worse. His name had been connected to a scandal involving contracts awarded to the Dayton-Wright Aircraft Company. Someone else would have to save Dayton aviation. This photograph, taken on July 4, 1923, shows one of McCook Field's last air shows. Proceeds from the show were donated to the Soldier's Emergency Relief Fund, a forerunner of today's Air Force Aid Society. (AFLCMC.)

Into the picture stepped John H. Patterson (seen on the right, around 1918), founder and chairman of National Cash Register (NCR). Patterson had long been a supporter of the Air Service and was a force to be reckoned with. Like Ed Deeds, Patterson had his own connections in Washington, DC, including Brig. Gen. Billy Mitchell (then assistant chief of the Air Service). Along with his only son, Lt. Frederick B. Patterson (left), the elder Patterson was determined to stop the Army's Engineering Division from leaving Dayton. (AFLCMC.)

Flying cadets from the Signal Corps Aviation School at Wilbur Wright Field enjoy a reception on the lawn of Far Hills, John H. Patterson's personal estate. Taken in 1918, this photograph shows Patterson's deep appreciation of the Air Service and its importance to the city of Dayton. (AFLCMC.)

John H. Patterson was one of Dayton's most successful and influential citizens. He knew how important McCook Field was to Dayton. Keeping the base meant a large number of federal jobs and long-term employment for Dayton's many aeronautical engineers. Patterson began talks with Billy Mitchell about aggressive steps to keep the base in town. He also sent two NCR representatives to Washington to lobby for more funding for the Air Service, hoping the money would be used for McCook Field's relocation. On May 5, 1922, Patterson and the Dayton Chamber of Commerce hosted a gala at the Gibbons Hotel to honor Mitchell and Colonel Bane, commanding officer of McCook Field. There, Patterson outlined his plans to keep the base in Dayton. Sadly, two days later, he died of heart failure on a train bound for Atlantic City. (AFLCMC.)

Upon John H. Patterson's death, his only son, Frederick B. Patterson (pictured), became chairman of NCR. During World War I, the younger Patterson was a second lieutenant in the Air Service, serving with the 15th Photographic Air Squadron in France. Patterson soon learned that the Army had decided to relocate the Engineering Division's test facility outside of Ohio. Several sites, including a large area in Michigan, were being offered to the Army for free. Patterson knew that any bid to keep the base in Dayton had to include the land upon which it would be built. He quickly organized and became president of the Dayton Air Service Committee, made up of 19 prominent Dayton citizens, including Ed Deeds. The committee selected a 4,988-acre site near the present town of Riverside as the offer. Stretched out over two counties, the site included 2,245 acres already leased by the Army for Wilbur Wright Field. The Army was paying $20,000 a year for this land. Patterson believed that giving the Army the land it was already leasing would be an offer it could not refuse. Of the 4,988 acres needed, 4,325 acres were owned by the Miami Conservancy District, while the remainder was distributed among seven privately owned parcels. Estimates showed that $325,000 would have to be raised to acquire all the land. (AFLCMC.)

On October 25, 1922, Frederick Patterson received word from Air Service officials that if the money could be raised, they would gladly accept his offer. Patterson had to act fast, as his option for the land expired on January 1, 1923. That evening, he convened a meeting of the Dayton Air Service Committee at the Dayton Country Club. The prominent business leaders, from left to right, are Irving G. Kumlar, H.W. Karr, G.W. Shroyer, Dr. D.F. Garland, Edward Wuichet, Frederick H. Rike, Patterson, W.R. Craven, John C. Haswell, H.D. Webrley, Valentine Winters, and John F. Ahlers. Seated at back right are Ezera M. Kuhns and Harold E. Talbott. (AFLCMC.)

On October 27, 1922, Frederick B. Patterson hosted a dinner for 200 team captains in the NCR dining room. There, he laid out the committee's fundraising plan. The goal was to raise $400,000, with another $25,000 set aside for a permanent memorial to the Wright brothers. On October 31, all of Dayton became aware of the campaign as factory whistles across the city went off at noon while demonstration flights from McCook Field soared over the city. (AFLCMC.)

DAYTON DAILY NEWS

72 PAGES TODAY

MAIN NEWS SECTION

VOL. XXXVIII. No. 363 (SUNDAY EDITION)   DAYTON, OHIO, SUNDAY, AUGUST 17, 1924.   PRICE FIVE CENTS

U. S. ACCEPTS AIR FIELD GIFT

Military Home May Have New Hospital

DAYTON LAUDED AS PATTERSON SUBMITS DEEDS

OLD STRUCTURE FOUND UNSAFE AS PROBE ENDS

MILLIONS TO BE SPENT HERE

PROPOSED NEW FLYING FIELD

DAYTON

M'COY FIGHTS SANITY PROBE OF ALIENISTS

ALLIED, GERMAN DELEGATES SIGN DEBT PROTOCOL

YOUTH OF LOEB LEOPOLD IS PUT TO FOREGROUND

MAN SHOT IN BOX CAR FIGHT

DAVIS TO MAKE 2 SPEECHES IN BUCKEYE STATE

Frederick B. Patterson's plan worked. By sundown on October 31, $278,573 had been pledged. By the second day, the campaign had already exceeded the committee's goal. The people of Dayton had shown their support far beyond anyone's expectations. The final total donated was $425,673. Once the donations were tallied, Patterson sent a telegraph to General Patrick that reads, in part: "The spirit which dominated this campaign will ever mark the attitude of Dayton toward the United States Air Service. Our citizens will always extend a hearty hand of fellowship toward its members. We are not unmindful of the kindly interest you have taken in this great project, and desire to thank you for your many courtesies and kind consideration. / With best wishes for the continued wonderful progress of the United States Air Service, and assurances that Dayton always may be depended upon to do its share in furthering such a splendid and necessary cause, we are / The Dayton Air Services Committee / F.B. Patterson, General Chairman." (AFLCMC.)

All 4,988 acres donated by the citizens of Dayton can be seen in this aerial photograph taken in the late 1960s. On August 21, 1925, the name Wilbur Wright Field was dropped by the War Department. The base was renamed Wright Field to honor both Wright brothers. The base is bordered to the south by the current town of Riverside, to the west by the Mad River and Huffman Dam, and to the east by the former towns of Fairfield and Osborn. On January 1, 1950, Fairfield and Osborn merged to create the town of Fairborn. On July 1, 1931, Wright Field was divided into two bases. Everything south of the Huffman Dam retained the name Wright Field, while the larger area north of the dam was renamed Patterson Field. In 1944, the Air Services Command Headquarters along Route 444 was given the designation Area A. Wright Field was designated Area B, while Patterson Field became Area C. In 2012, the designation Area C was dropped, and Areas A and C were finally reunited after 70 years. (AFLCMC.)

Ground-breaking ceremonies for Wright Field were held on April 16, 1926. More than 100 citizens of Dayton were on hand for the ceremony, including members of the Dayton Air Service Committee, Orville and Katharine Wright, and military officials from McCook Field, Wilbur Wright Field, and the Fairfield Air Depot. Standing are, from left to right, G.H. Shroyer, E.C. Berry, Howard Smith, Joseph McKenny, C.E. Comer, R.J. Hutchinson, I.G. Kumler, George B. Smith, Maj. Augustine W. Robins (Fairfield Air Depot commander), Capt. E.M. George, Orville Wright, Frederick B. Patterson, George W. Lane, Lt. Lester Maitland (McCook Field test pilot), Maj. J.F. Curry (McCook Field Engineering Division chief), W.M. Brock, Howard Egbert, John Ahlers, U.C. Thies, E.A. Johnson, and T.C. McMahon. (AFLCMC.)

On the morning of March 25, 1927 the first trucks arrived to begin the relocation of McCook Field to Wright Field. A total of 69 buildings were to be salvaged or razed. Smaller wooden buildings could be lifted onto flatbed trucks, while larger steel buildings were dismantled. In the end, over 4,500 tons of material was salvaged and moved to Wright Field, including 1,052 steel file cabinets, 600 desks, hundreds of toilets and sinks, thousands of doors, windows, and frames, and 900 tons of steel worth over $81,000 that was salvaged from McCook's hangers (pictured). The move took over two years to complete. McCook Field's Propeller Test Rig was the last facility to relocate, finally moving to Wright Field on May 22, 1929. (Both, AFLCMC.)

Katharine and Orville Wright (center, facing left) attended the Wright Field ground-breaking ceremony, accompanied by officers from McCook Field. The ceremony was one of the last times the siblings appeared together in public. In November 1926, Katharine married newspaperman Henry J. Haskell, a widower whom she had dated in college. Orville was devastated and broke off all contact with her. She would not be present for Wright Field's dedication on October 12, 1927. (AFLCMC.)

A steam shovel was provided for the symbolic ground breaking, and several of the dignitaries in attendance took turns operating it. The first to break ground was Frederick B. Patterson, who had organized the campaign to keep the Air Service in Dayton. He was followed by Maj. John F. Curry, commander of McCook Field, and Maj. Augustine Warner Robins, commander of the Fairfield Air Depot. (AFLCMC.)

Wright Field's garages are pictured under construction around 1926, with warehouses and the water tower in the background. The entrance to the steam pipe tunnel is in the foreground. Today, these buildings are known collectively as Building 51. (NMUSAF.)

Wright Field's receiving warehouses are seen under construction in these photographs from late 1926. Located along the base's railroad line, they were intended to receive and store supplies arriving by train. By the late 1940s, railroad deliveries had switched to Area C, and these buildings were converted for testing equipment under stressful conditions and, later, gasoline explosion testing. In the 1980s, the laboratory areas were converted into office space for the KC-10 and T-46A Directorates, as well as offices of the Defense Nuclear Agency. Collectively known as Building 56, they recently housed the F-15 System Program Office—not too shabby for buildings originally intended as warehouses. (NMUSAF.)

One of most historic buildings in the Air Force's inventory, Wright Field's Assembly Building (Building 31) is seen in this 1931 photograph. Built to replace McCook Field's much smaller assembly building, this Assembly Building left no doubt that the Army Air Service was in Dayton to stay. Building 31 was one of several aircraft testing laboratories located at Wright Field. They included the Structures Development and Test Laboratory, the Propeller Research and Test Laboratory, and the Aerodynamics Research and Test Laboratory. Collectively, they formed the most advanced aircraft test facility in the world. The Assembly Building was large enough to accommodate even the biggest bombers in service at the time. From 1927 until the end of World War II, nearly every type of aircraft tested by the US Army Air Forces visited this hangar at one time or another. Building 31 now houses Wright-Patterson's landing gear and wheel testing facility. Employing the world's largest dynamometer for testing tires, virtually all military and civilian landing gear systems have been tested here, including the space shuttles' tires. (AFLCMC.)

With a view looking northwest, the above photograph shows the Wright Field Laboratory Building (Building 16) under construction. Built to house all of the various Materials Branch Testing Labs, it is the largest structure (at 295,935 square feet) ever erected at Wright Field. The basement's first tenant was the Psychological Research Laboratory. In 1934, a high-altitude test chamber was installed, which was used by Wiley Post to test his pressure suits. Maj. Carl Greene and Maj. John Younger developed America's first pressurized airplane cabin for the Lockheed XC-35 in Building 16, and the Explorer 1 gondola used by Capt. Al Stevens in his 1934 world altitude record attempt was constructed here. In 1934, a WPA project was undertaken to dig a basement for the building. With workers digging by hand, one section at a time, the basement was completed in 1939. (Both, NMUSAF.)

Seen in this image from March 1927, the Administration Building (Building 11) was the first structure completed at Wright Field. Construction began on June 30, 1926, and was completed on April 12, 1927. Erected as headquarters for Air Materials Command, Building 11 was the most important headquarters in the Army Air Corps. Personnel in the 550-by-55-foot building oversaw all aircraft research and development, engineering, flight-testing, procurement, field service, industrial war plans, and repair and maintenance. The decisions to produce many famous aircraft, such as the P-38 Lightning, P-51 Mustang, and B-17 Flying Fortress, were made in this building. (NMUSAF.)

Above each of Building 11's twin entrances are identical porcelain shields designed by C.P. Johnson of Cincinnati. They depict Auguste Rodin's *The Thinker* studying a winged globe. Originally designed for the Engineering Division at McCook Field, they became the shield of the Air Corps Materiel Division when it was formed in 1926. (AFLCMC.)

Taken on June 3, 1927, this photograph shows the conditions at Wright Field around the time personnel began arriving. Since March 25, equipment belonging to the Materiel Division had been arriving from McCook Field by way of truck and rail. By the time the move was completed, over 4,500 tons of equipment had been relocated, including 900 tons of steel from dismantled buildings at McCook. By June, the Administration Building (foreground) and the Laboratories Building (behind) were occupied, but there was still much work left to be done. The unpaved streets had no lighting or sidewalks, and the base still lacked aircraft hangars, a boiler house, and a guard shack. Because the flying field was not yet ready, pilots and planes from the Flight Test Branch were temporary relocated to the Fairfield Air Depot. (AFLCMC.)

Because construction of base housing had not begun when these photographs were taken on June 3, 1927 (above), and June 1, 1927 (below), staff at Wright Field were forced to commute to work from rented houses around Dayton. Worse, work was frequently curtailed due to a lack of funds and personnel. Budget cuts for military aviation caused many talented engineers and scientists to leave for more lucrative jobs. Austerity measures meant vacancies could not be filled. As they arrived at their new facilities, many highly skilled scientists found themselves helping their lab technicians assemble lab hoods, benches, work stands, and room partitions. (Above, AFLCMC; below, NMUSAF.)

Wright Field received its first distinguished visitor before it even opened. On June 17, 1927, Charles A. Lindbergh flew over Wright Field while returning home from the first successful solo transatlantic flight. Five days later, Lindbergh flew back to Dayton. Area B was not yet ready, so he landed at the Fairfield Air Depot (Area C). Lindbergh is still wearing his flight cap as he talks with Brig. Gen. William E. Gilmore. Orville Wright is seated next to him. Lindbergh was driven to Wright's home, Hawthorn Hill, where he spent the night. (NMUSAF.)

On June 23, 1927, Orville Wright and Charles A. Lindbergh returned to Wright Field (Area B), where the pair received a grand tour of the unfinished base from Brig. Gen. William E. Gillmore (center), chief of the Air Corps Materiel Division. Wright (left) and Lindbergh (right) became good friends. During his visit, Lindbergh encouraged Wright to write an autobiography of his life with his brother. He started one but never completed it. (Author's collection.)

The dedication of Wright Field took place on the morning of October 12, 1927. Rain forced the event into the auditorium of the new Administration Building (Building 11). The ceremony, which began at 12:30 p.m., established three Army precedents. It marked the first time an Army installation had been named for two civilians who had never served in the military, the first time an installation had been named for a living individual, and the first time an individual was present at the dedication of a facility named for him. Orville Wright was given a place of honor onstage, though he declined to speak. (AFLCMC.)

Following the ceremony, the distinguished guests were photographed on the front steps of Building 11. Identified are, from left to right, (first row) Orville Wright, Secretary of War Dwight Davis, Judge Kenesaw Mountain Landis, Air Secretary F. Trubee Davison, and Maj. Gen. Mason M. Patrick (Army Air Corps chief); (second row) Brig. Gen William E. Gillmore (Materiel Division chief), Dr. Joseph Ames, and Col. Edward A. Deeds. (AFLCMC.)

An "Official Message from the Chief, Materiel Division" reads: "The establishment of a permanent home for the headquarters of the Materiel Division, and suitable laboratories for prosecuting the engineering and scientific work necessary in procuring satisfactory flying and fighting equipment for our Air Corps, is a matter that should react with general pride and satisfaction to all people of our great country, and in particular the people of Dayton, who through their generosity and understanding cooperation have helped to make these plans possible. / It is a fortuitous circumstance that the magnificent tract of land given to the government by the citizens of Dayton, should also be the scene of the first flying experiments of Wilbur and Orville Wright. / It is particularly fitting that this historic site should for all time be devoted to further experimentation in aviation, and maintained as an active and useful monument to their great gift to mankind. The dedication of this field in honor of the Wright Brothers, and of the people of Dayton who presented the site to the Government, should be splendid inspiration to the men who must carry on this important work, which in spite of the wonderful progress made in the near past, is but in its infancy. / It is pleasing to think that the name of Wright, in addition to the glory already won, will hereafter be directly associated with the future developments of aviation. / William E. Gillmore, Brigadier General, Air Corps, Chief, Materiel Division." (AFLCMC.)

While the speeches were being delivered inside, a ceremonial cannon was set up near the flagpole in front of the Administration Building. Once all the distinguished guests had emerged from the auditorium, it fired a single shot, signifying that Wright Field was officially open for business. (NMUSAF.)

As the flag was raised, members of the 10th Infantry Band, Ohio National Guard, played the national anthem in front of the Administration Building. When the flag reached the top of the pole, a 21-gun salute was fired. (AFLCMC.)

Following the speeches and the firing of the cannon, Orville Wright agreed to raise the first American flag over Wright Field. The ceremonial cannon was removed, and the distinguished guests crossed a wooden bridge over the mud to the flagpole in front of the Administration Building. There, Wright raised the flag while the Army band played the national anthem. The photograph above was taken at the conclusion of the flag raising. Wright is at center, retrieving his hat from Secretary of War Dwight Davis. The photograph below shows the huge flag as it waves above a line of parked cars. (Above, AFLCMC; below, NMUSAF.)

Although it had been announced that the mornings rains had caused the flying portion of the ceremony to be canceled, clearing skies led officials to reverse that decision. The show opened with aerobatic flying by several former McCook Field test pilots, including Lts. James Doolittle, James Hutchinson, and Reuben Moffat. Following a demonstration where an unmanned observation balloon was shot down in flames, 24 Curtiss P-1 Hawk pursuit planes of the 1st Pursuit Group from Selfridge Field in Michigan flew demonstrations of formation flying (above). The planes had arrived at the Fairfield Air Depot the previous day, and had spent the morning on public display. They were followed by parachute jumps made by M.H. Clair of Wright Field, and F.G. Manson, William Moore, and Owen Kindred of the Fairfield Air Depot (below). The day's activities concluded with the John L. Mitchell Trophy Race. Fifteen pilots of the 1st Pursuit Group competed in their P-1 Hawks, with Lt. I.A. Woodring taking home the trophy for the year. (He became a test pilot, and was killed when the Consolidated XA-11 (s/n 32-322) broke up over Wright Field on January 20, 1933.) (Both, AFLCMC.)

The Dynamometer Laboratory and the wind tunnels were two of the last three facilities to relocate to Wright Field, remaining in operation at McCook Field until 1929. McCook's 14-inch wind tunnel was constructed from 2,100 pieces of walnut taken from propeller trimmings. Nearly 22 feet long, it was capable of producing an airspeed of 453 miles per hour at its 14-inch choke point. It was used to test instruments and small aircraft models. Today, it is on display at the National Museum of the US Air Force. (AFLCMC.)

Constructed in 1921, McCook Field's five-foot wind tunnel was designed to test models too large for the 14-inch tunnel. Working without any detailed designs, the woodshop at McCook Field constructed it in just over a year. The wind tunnel measures 96 feet long and five feet in diameter at the choke point, and its two counter-rotating 12-foot, 12-bladed fans produce airspeeds of up to 260 miles per hour. It was relocated to Wright Field in 1929, where its spectacular career has spanned from testing the Barling Bomber in the early 1920s to tests of the Lockheed C-130 Hercules, Boeing EC-135, McDonnell F-4C Phantom II, and McDonnell Douglas F-15 Eagle. Today, it is the oldest operating wind tunnel in the world. (AFLCMC.)

Completed in early 1929, the first wind tunnel building at Wright Field was designed only as a temporary structure. It allowed McCook Field's 5-foot and 14-inch wind tunnels to finally be relocated to Wright Field. By the time they arrived a more permanent structure (Building 19) was already under construction. (AFLCMC.)

In late 1929, the five-foot wind tunnel was relocated to its permanent home inside Building 19, which was constructed of brick to stabilize internal air pressure. From 1922 until the 1970s, virtually every new aircraft design was tested here, including most World War II Army Air Corps aircraft. In 1958, the wind tunnel was turned over to the Air Force Institute of Technology, which continues to operate it as a teaching and research tool. In 1992, the American Society of Mechanical Engineers dedicated it as a National Historic Mechanical Engineering Landmark. (AFLCMC.)

The last facility to move from McCook Field was the Propeller Test Rig, which finally relocated to Wright Field on May 22, 1929. Designed to test wooden propellers, the McCook Field test rig consisted of a bombproof control room, onto which the propeller was mounted, and a protective shroud to catch the flying debris. The introduction of metal propellers in the 1920s made it necessary to develop a much more powerful and sophisticated system for testing propellers at Wright Field. (NMUSAF.)

When completed, Wright Field's Propeller Research and Test Laboratory was the largest and most powerful in the world. Three concrete test rigs can accommodate propellers of up to 45 feet in diameter. Electric motors of up to 6,000 horsepower enabled propeller endurance tests at speeds up to 4,300 revolutions per minute. When the propeller lab and the power plant lab conducted tests, their demand for electricity was so great that a special Dispatcher's Office at Wright Field was established to coordinate testing schedules with Dayton Power and Light. Thousands of hours of propeller tests at Wright Field led to the development of controllable-speed and variable-speed propellers. The propeller test rigs were soon enclosed due to the horrific noise they produced. (AFLCMC.)

The Power Plant Branch's Torque Stand laboratory was completed in 1929. It housed seven 40-foot stacks connected by a passageway (six for engine endurance tests and one for propeller testing). Each stack was open on top to allow fresh air in and to pass discharged air upward. Engines submitted to the Army for testing were subjected to a 150-hour type test. The sound generated by the testing was so deafening that pilots flying 600 feet over the building were unable to hear their own engines. (AFLCMC.)

Refrigeration equipment in the Power Plant Branch's laboratory was used to develop low-temperature controls for aircraft, as well as cold weather accessories. It was also employed in the testing of an antifreeze solution called Prestone. Prestone's efficiency allowed the size of aircraft radiators to be reduced by 60 percent, making possible the development of inline liquid-cooled engines, like the Allison and Merlin engines of World War II. Research by Wright Field's Power Plant Branch allowed the US Army to develop more streamlined high-performance liquid-cooled engines for fighter aircraft, while the Navy continued to rely on larger air-cooled radial engines. (AFLCMC.)

One of Wright Field's first tasks was finding a replacement for the Army's aging Curtiss P-1C Hawk pursuit planes. The P-1 Hawks were the first Army aircraft to carry the "P" designation and were the Army's standard pursuit biplanes in 1927. Powered by a 435-horsepower Curtiss D-12E engine with a top speed of 155 miles per hour, the P-1C pictured was among the last of the P-1 series, which had been in production since 1925. To replace them, the Materiel Division issued a request for a pursuit plane capable of 225 miles per hour at 15,000 feet. (AFLCMC.)

This photograph displays the synchronized gun installation on a Curtiss P-1C Hawk. Already outdated, this aircraft was among the last group of 33 P-1C Hawks delivered in April 1929. The Hawk's twin .30-caliber Browning machine guns are aimed through a simple ring mounted on the cowling. The last P-1C was withdrawn from active service in 1930. (AFLCMC.)

The Curtiss Company's design for the competition, the XP-10, was also likely the first prototype to begin its flight-testing at Wright Field. The Curtiss XP-10 arrived at Wright Field in August 1928 and first flew in September. Like its competitor, the Boeing XP-9, the Curtiss XP-10 was powered by a 600-horsepower Curtiss V-1570 V-12 engine, giving it a top speed of 173 miles per hour. When Boeing's design was grounded after just 15 hours of flying, Curtiss had high hopes that the XP-10 would soon replace its P-1 Hawks in service. The XP-10 featured many innovations, including all-plywood wings in place of wood and fabric and upper gull wings joined at the fuselage to enhance pilot visibility, and reduce drag. To eliminate the bulky front radiator, Curtiss developed an unusual cooling system made of corrugated brass sheets mounted to the upper wings. They improved performance but were very susceptible to enemy fire. Though its performance figures were promising, the airplane was not ordered into production. (AFLCMC.)

After testing at Wright Field in 1929 found neither the Boeing XP-9 nor Curtiss XP-10 suitable for production, the Army turned to the Navy's Boeing F4B. Testing of a Navy plane showed such promise that it was ordered into production without a prototype. The first flight of an updated XP-12A took place at Wright Field on April 11, 1929, but the airplane was destroyed in a midair collision on May 18, after just four hours of flying. Despite the accident, it was ordered into production as the P-12A. Pictured is a later model P-12C undergoing flight tests at Wright Field in early 1930. (AFLCMC.)

The Boeing P-12 series proved to be one of the Army Air Corps' most successful aircraft, remaining in service from 1929 until 1941. It was the first American-built pursuit plane with an all-metal monocoque fuselage and the Army's last pursuit biplane. In total, Boeing produced 366 P-12s— flown by more young officers who would become generals than any other airplane. It is also the aircraft killing King Kong. Many lessons learned flying the P-12 were applied to American combat aircraft in World War II. (AFLCMC.)

1929 WRIGHT FLYERS
First Flying Nin

In 1929, McCook Field's baseball team moved to Wright Field and became the Wright Flyers. Seen here in 1929 in front of a Ford C-4 transport (an Army version of the venerable Ford Trimotor), the Flyers won the Cosmopolitan League Championship with a 13-2 record in their first year at Wright Field. (AFLCMC.)

Two

THE AIR CORPS
ENGINEERING SCHOOL
TO TRAIN AIR CORPS OFFICERS IN THE
HIGHER PHASES OF
AERONAUTICAL ENGINEERING

In 1919, the Air Service Engineering School was established at McCook Field. The Army wanted to shift research, development, and even construction of new military aircraft out of the private sector as much as possible and place it under the control of Army engineers. The Air School of Applications was established in 1919 at McCook Field to provide a pipeline of qualified officers to undertake and supervise aircraft design and production. The first class was held in a hangar on November 10, 1919, under the supervision of Lt. Edwin E. Aldrin Sr., who had recently graduated with a master's degree in aeronautical engineering from the Massachusetts Institute of Technology (MIT). The first graduation ceremony was held in September 1920. When McCook Field moved to Wright Field in 1927, the Air Corps Engineering School (as it was renamed in 1920) went with it, moving initially into the Materiel Division Headquarters Building (Building 11). However, a change in attitude had occurred in the 1920s. With money scarce, aircraft manufacturers starved for contracts began complaining that aircraft designed and built by the Materiel Division were hurting their ability to produce military aircraft on a larger scale. Maj. Gen. Mason M. Patrick agreed, and by the time the school reopened at Wright Field, the Army Air Corps was no longer designing and producing its own aircraft. As a result, the Air Corps had to rely on private firms for new aircraft. From that change emerged the need for the Army Proposal Circular, a detailed description of the type of aircraft the Air Corps desired, with requirements for speed, range, weapons, and load carrying capabilities. In September 1946, the Air Corps Engineering School was renamed the Army Air Forces Institute of Technology. On July 16, 1948, it then became the USAF Institute of Technology (AFIT). By 2014, it had awarded over 20,000 graduate degrees and grown into three graduate schools with six departments, as well as a Civilian Institution Program (CIP) that helps officers and enlisted personnel gain graduate degrees from hundreds of civilian colleges and universities worldwide.

The first class of the Air Service Engineering School graduated in September 1920. Those pictured are identified as, from left to right, (standing) Mr. LaBale (instructor), Lieutenant Wilcox, Major Frank, Colonel McIntosh, and Private Perkins; (seated) Lieutenant Aldrin, Colonel Benedict, Colonel Rader, and Major Sneed. Lt. Edwin E. "Gene" Aldrin Sr. ran the school until 1922. Aldrin attended Clark University, studying under Robert Goddard, who encouraged him to pursue a career in aviation. After earning a master's degree in aeronautical engineering from MIT, Aldrin married Marion Moon, and the couple had two daughters and a son. On July 21, 1969, their son, Edwin E. "Buzz" Aldrin Jr., became the second man to walk on the moon. (AFLCMC.)

In this image taken in 1922, Air Service Engineering School students are seen conducting a test using the McCook Field wind tunnel. Among the school's early graduates were many famous pilots, including Lt. James H. "Jimmy" Doolittle, Lt. Harold R. Harris, Capt. George C. Kenney, and Lt. John A. Macready. Doolittle and Macready graduated together in 1923. Macready won the Mackay Trophy three consecutive times, while Doolittle led the B-25 raid on Tokyo in 1942. (AFLCMC.)

In 1927, the Air Corps Engineering School moved to Wright Field. Classes were held in Building 11. In 1935, the school moved to Building 12, where it operated until 1939 and briefly from August to December 1941. Here, students of the class of 1929 pose in front of Building 11. They are, from left to right, (first row) Lt. George Tourtellot, Lt. Clements McMullen, Maj. Adelai M. Gilkeson, Capt. Hubert V. Hopkins, Lt. Harold N. Carr, and Lt. Muir S. Fairchild; (second row) Lts. Charles W. Caldwell, Alfred A. Kessler, Jr., George F. Schulgen, James G. Taylor, and John W. Bowman. (AFLCMC.)

Col. George V. Holloman was a graduate of the class of 1935. In 1937, he received the Mackay Trophy for pioneering the world's first automated landing. In April 1941, Major Holloman was placed in charge of a new group of laboratories at Wright Field known as the Special Weapons Group, where he worked on remotely guided aircraft. In March 1945, he was transferred to a secret assignment in the South Pacific. He was killed in a B-17 crash in Formosa (now Taiwan) on March 19, 1946. Today, Holloman Air Force Base is named in his honor. He is pictured working on a Q-2 radar-controlled target drone. (AFLCMC.)

World War II put Wright Field into high gear. With resources and personnel at a premium, the Air Corps Engineering School was closed for 17 months, beginning in 1939. Reopening as the Army Air Forces Engineering School on August 1, 1941, it closed again on December 9, following the attack on Pearl Harbor. It did not reopen until March 17, 1944. The class of 44B is seen in front of a temporary classroom. Wartime demand for base facilities forced the school to move into wooden barracks located on the other side of Springfield Street. (AFLCMC.)

In this 1947 photograph, students of the Army Air Forces Institute of Technology are seen in front of Wright Field's five-foot wind tunnel, holding an early swept-wing model. On July 16, 1948, the school's name was changed to the USAF Institute of Technology (now AFIT). With the enrollment of Lt. Col. Mary J. Strong in September 1958, the school was officially coed, but its facilities were still scattered around the base. On December 18, 1962, Gen. Curtiss LeMay broke ground for the school's long-anticipated $4 million School of Engineering building. By 2014, AFIT had awarded over 20,000 degrees, and over 400,000 students have enrolled in its continuing education programs. (AFLCMC.)

Three

THE 1930S
FASTER, HIGHER, FARTHER

In World War II, airpower brought German industry to its knees and reduced Japan's cities to ashes, but the aircraft that fought in World War II were almost all developed and tested at Wright Field in the 1930s. By 1935, the interval between an airplane design being accepted for development and it entering service was three to five years, meaning that the aircraft the Army Air Service had on hand at the start of World War II were all tested at Wright Field in the mid-1930s, and most aircraft entering service as the war came to a close were already in development by 1941.

During the 1930s, Wright Field served as the Army Air Service's "nerve center" for aircraft research and development. When the Air Service wanted a new airplane, the Materiel Division would issue an Army Proposal Circular to aircraft manufacturers. The circular would specify the desired speed, range, and payload capacity for the aircraft. Manufacturers would fly their prototypes to Wright Field under civilian registration, where each entry was thoroughly tested. If an aircraft failed to complete the testing or crashed, it was eliminated from consideration, even if Wright Field staff were at fault. Once the winning design was chosen, the prototype was purchased and assigned an "X" or "Y1" designation. The staff at Wright Field then worked alongside the airplane's manufacturer to assist in its final development before determining how many aircraft to buy when all requirements had been met. Once the airplane was in service, the staff at Wright Field continued to supervise the aircraft's operations to make sure it was fulfilling all its duties. Modification orders were issued when problems arose, or termination of the contract if the aircraft was not meeting expectations. During World War II, no other country had such a centralized system for aircraft development, acquisition, and management. Today, Wright Field's model serves as a template for other nations' air force operations. But in the 1930s, Wright Field's unique organizational system gave the United States a significant advantage in developing the aircraft used in World War II.

Wright Field's two stone gatehouses were completed in late September 1931. Originally located on Springfield Street near Building 11, they had attached stone walls displaying the base's name. In the 1990s, both gatehouses were dismantled when the base's main entrance was moved further south. They were rebuilt at the new entrance, though further from the road, and the walls were eliminated. (AFLCMC.)

The Wright Field aircraft operations center was located in Hangar 3. All flight plans and crew assignments were made at the operations center, which oversaw both experimental flight-testing and active duty squadrons. The aircraft operations center opened in 1929 and remained in Hanger 3 until 1943, when it moved to Building 8. (AFLCMC.)

As Wright Field neared completion, aircraft development and testing quickly accelerated. Taken on November 11, 1930, this photograph shows workers from the Airplane Branch riveting a flat covering to the wing of the Lockheed Y1C-12 (s/n 31-405) Vega. The Y1C-12 was likely the first airplane evaluated at Wright Field with a fully cantilevered wing (internal bracing only). (AFLCMC.)

Photographed at Wright Field on October 2, 1930, the Lockheed Y1C-12 Vega was designed by Jack Northrop, who would go on to form his own aircraft company. The Y1C-12 was evaluated at Wright Field in 1930. Engineers were impressed with its speed and lack of external bracing. The Vega featured a fully monocoque fuselage (no internal supports) and cantilevered wings (no external bracing). The sole Y1C-12 was purchased by the Army Air Corps in 1931 and operated as a light, fast transport until scrapped in 1935. (NMUSAF.)

Taken on April 3, 1931, this photograph shows the first Curtiss XA-8 Shrike (30-387) shortly after it arrived at Wright Field for evaluation. Designed for ground attack, the Shrike won a 1930 competition to replace the Air Service's aging attack biplanes. Powered by an inline Curtiss V-1570 engine, the all-metal Shrike had a top speed of 196 miles per hour, faster than most pursuit planes of the time. Produced in small numbers, they remained in service until 1940. The Curtiss A-8 Shrike was the first modern ground attack aircraft, a forerunner of the Republic A-10 Thunderbolt II "Warthog." (NMUSAF.)

In an excellent example of the role the Armament Division played in the development of new aircraft, this photograph, taken on August 24, 1931, shows crewmen loading 25-pound bombs into the Shrike's vertical bomb bays. In addition to developing new guns and bombs, the Armament Division was also responsible for designing new ways to mount them—a task no less important then the weapons themselves. (NMUSAF.)

The XA-8 Shrike was a very modern airplane for its time. It featured a fully enclosed cockpit and a semi-enclosed rear gunner's station. Taken on August, 24, 1931, this photograph shows the Shrike's rear-mounted M-2 .30-caliber machine gun. Curtiss originally designed the Shrike with an open rear gunner's station. It was redesigned, with a new gun mount added by Wright Field's Armament Division prior to the aircraft entering production. (NMUSAF.)

The XA-8 Shrike was intended for ground attack. It featured two forward-firing M-2 .30-caliber machine guns mounted inside each wheel fairing. In addition to giving the aircraft significant forward firepower, placing the guns inside the wheel fairings kept them outside of the propeller's arc. Today, the Republic A-10 Warthog uses a single General Electric GAU-8/A Avenger 30-millimeter gun mounted in the nose for the same purpose. (NMUSAF.)

The purpose of Wright Field was not only to evaluate new aircraft but also to improve them wherever possible. Once all the branches had finished working on it, an aircraft often bore little resemblance to the one that had arrived. The original Douglas XO-25A is pictured above on July 17, 1931. The photograph below shows the same aircraft (s/n 30-160) on December 15, 1931, after the Power Plant Branch had replaced the original water-cooled radiator with one that used Prestone, reducing radiator size by 60 percent. The smaller radiator allowed the Airplane Branch to develop a new, more streamlined nose with a smaller propeller and a pointed spinner cap. Development of the O-25 continued until the plane was lost in a crash at March Field, California, on December 1, 1932, killing pilot Frank D. Hackett. (Both, AFLCMC.)

On July 7, 1929, the Keystone B-3A bomber arrived at Wright Field for testing. The testing of bombers had begun in 1928 with six prototypes, but none showed promise. The B-3A was the fist significant improvement of World War I bombers. It featured twin 525-horsepower Pratt & Whitney R-1690-A engines, giving it a top speed of 114 miles per hour. It had a crew of four and could carry 2,500 pounds of bombs. Although the prototype was wrecked at Wright Field on November 12, 1929, the aircraft was ordered into production. Pictured is the first production B-3A (s/n 30-281), which was delivered in October 1930. By 1931, it had become the standard Air Corps bomber. (NMUSAF.)

Dynamic testing of the Keystone B-3A at Wright Field is shown in this 1929 image. The aircraft pictured is actually the prototype LB-10 (s/n 29-27). The airplane is suspended in preparation for a 6-inch drop to test the landing gear. Structural testing of landing gear and tires was an integral part of Wright Field's mission and continues to this day. Nearly 50 years later, the tires for the space shuttle were tested just a few hundred feet from where this photograph was taken. (NMUSAF.)

In 1930, the Air Corps began looking for an all-metal monoplane bomber to replace the aging B-3A. Five designs were submitted. The Douglas XB-7 arrived at Wright Field in July 1932. The XB-7 was a modified version of Douglas's XO-35 observation plane, with bomb racks installed under the fuselage. Because the XO-35 was nearing production, an order for an additional seven Y1B-7 bombers was placed as well, making the Y1B-7 the first monoplane to carry the "B" designation for "bomber." When the Army took over airmail service in 1934, all seven Y1B-7 were used as mail carriers in western states, resulting in the loss of four. The last was stricken in December 1938. (NMUSAF.)

In this early 1932 photograph, a Boeing B-9 bomber is seen flying over the Dayton area, accompanied by a Boeing P-26 Peashooter pursuit plane. Both the Y1B-9 and Douglas Y1B-7 were ordered into production, though only five Boeing B-9 bombers were ever produced. Although the B-9s were faster than most pursuit aircraft at the time, the Martin B-10 bomber was nearing production and promised even greater performance. Note the Wright Field "spearhead" insignia on the sides of both aircraft. (NMUSAF.)

The Martin B-907 arrived at Wright Field on March 20, 1932. It featured an enclosed cockpit and a box cantilever wing designed by the Materiel Division at Wright Field. Flight tests revealed a top speed of 196 miles per hour. After some modifications, it was returned to Wright Field in November 1933 with twin 775-horsepower Wright 1820-33 engines, an internal bomb bay, and a power-operated nose turret. In testing, it achieved a remarkable speed of 207 miles per hour. Fitted with the first Norden bombsights, it was ordered into production as the Martin B-10. These photographs show a prototype YB-12 during flight-testing at Wright Field in April 1934. The B-12 used more powerful Pratt & Whitney R-1690-11 engines. The B-10 was so advanced it made all other bombers obsolete. No pursuit plane could catch it. It remains one of the most significant aircraft ever tested at Wright Field. (Above, AFLCMC; below, NMUSAF.)

On July 19, 1934, the former commander of the Fairfield Aviation General Supply Depot, Lt. Col. Henry "Hap" Arnold, led a formation of 10 Martin B-10 bombers on an 8,290-mile round-trip flight between Bolling Field, Washington, DC, and Fairbanks, Alaska. The flight demonstrated America's ability to protect its overseas possessions by air, as well as the rugged durability of the B-10 bomber. For his accomplishment, Arnold (standing at center) received the Mackay Trophy and the Distinguished Flying Cross. (NMUSAF.)

The only surviving Martin B-10 is now on display at the National Museum of the US Air Force. The aircraft was an export model sold to Argentina in 1938 and was still being used as an instructional airframe in the 1960s. In 1970, Argentina donated it to the US government. The aircraft was restored by the 96th Maintenance Squadron at Kelly Air Force Base in the markings of a B-10 from the 1934 Alaskan flight. This 1976 photograph shows the plane's unveiling ceremony at the Air Force Museum. (NMUSAF.)

This remarkable photograph shows what Wright Field (Area B) looked like in October 1934. Hangars 2, 3, 4, and 10 (the headhouse) are clearly visible, as are Parking Sheds 1, 2, and 3, just behind them. The mysterious Hangar 1 was deemed unsuitable before construction began and was never built, though over the years a popular prank was sending newly arriving airmen to deliver a message there. The concrete apron is completed, with a circular Compass Swing Base on the bottom right corner. Scattered around the apron is an amazing collection of early pursuit planes, transport aircraft, and bombers, including what is almost certainly the Martin B-907 parked in the Compass Swing Base. The B-907 was the prototype for the revolutionary Martin B-10 bomber series that would serve in air forces around the world until World War II. It was tested at Wright Field from 1932 to 1934. Wright Field's baseball diamond was located just below the Compass Swing Base. The small building just across the road is the gas station. Behind it are the Torque Stand Building (Building 71) and the original Wind Tunnel Building (Building 22). On the far right is the Propeller Test Laboratory (Building 20, above) and the Armament Test Laboratory and Gun Range (Building 21, below). It is interesting to note the fields of freshly harvested hay visible at the bottom of the photograph. Much of today's Wright-Patterson Air Force Base was still farmland until World War II. (AFLCMC.)

Not all aircraft tested at Wright Field were as successful as the Martin B-10. Seen here is the Bell XFM-1 Airacuda, possibly the worst aircraft ever produced for the Army Air Corps. The XFM-1 (Fighter Multiplace) was designed to intercept incoming bombers over the Atlantic. It was powered by two Allison V-1710-9 engines driving pusher propellers, and was armed with two 37-millimeter cannon located inside gunners' stations on the front of each engine nacelle. The XFM-1 arrived at Wright Field in the fall of 1937, and was soon found to be seriously underpowered. It was unstable in flight, its twin pusher engines were prone to overheating, and the cannons filled the gunners' stations with smoke when fired. Although the Airacuda featured many innovations, including the first auxiliary power unit (APU) ever installed on an airplane, its unreliability made it dangerous to fly. The XFM-1 was sent back to Bell, which pressed ahead with development despite the plane's many drawbacks. Taken on November 5, 1937, this photograph shows Wright Field test pilot Lt. B.F. Kelsey flying the XFM-1 over the Dayton area. (Author's collection.)

Possibly the rarest photographs in this book, these images were taken at Patterson Field in 1940. They show the first Bell YFM-1 Airacuda (39-486) following conversion to a YFM-1B. The Airacuda were frequent visitors to Wright Field, as the Air Corps struggled to make something usable out of them. By the time production ended in 1940, a total of 13 Airacudas had been produced in four different versions. Two were converted to YFM-1B by switching to Allison V-1710-41 engines without turbosuperchargers. These are the only known photographs showing an Airacuda in Wright Field markings. The Airacuda never entered squadron service; by the end of 1942, all 13 had been scrapped. (Both, author's collection.)

Building 12, the Technical Data Building (above), opened to the public in 1935. Perhaps the most beautiful building at Wright Field, it is an Art Deco masterpiece. Constructed during the Depression by the Works Progress Administration (WPA), it cost $235,000. Built to house the Army Aeronautical Museum, as well as offices for the Technical Data Branch, it features a rotunda with green marble floors, wood paneling, and a second-floor balcony (below). An Art Deco clock in the shape of pilot's wings hangs over the main entrance, while bronze busts of Orville and Wilbur Wright grace the sides. The museum opened on February 17, 1936, but wartime demands forced its closure on May 27, 1940. From 1935 until 1941, the Air Corps Engineering School was located in Building 12. Renamed Monahan Hall on March 30, 1993, Building 12 underwent a full restoration in 2009, winning a merit award in 2010 from the Ohio State Historic Preservation Office. (Both, AFLCMC.)

The Army Aeronautical Museum, pictured in the late 1930s, was the predecessor of today's Air Force Museum. Opening in 1923 at McCook Field, it contained a collection of World War I–era aircraft and artifacts. In 1932, it moved briefly into Building 11 at Wright Field, before relocating to Building 12, where it reopened on February 17, 1936. When Building 12 was constructed, it was the nation's only air museum and the first building in the United States designed for that purpose. Sadly, the onset of World War II forced the museum's closure on May 27, 1940. In August 1954, the Air Force Museum reopened in Building 89 in Area C, before moving in 1971 to its current location in Building 489 in Area B. (AFLCMC.)

The reading room of the Technical Branch Library in Building 12 is pictured here in the early 1950s. The Technical Data Branch was responsible for assembling and disseminating aeronautical information. Employing a staff of scriptwriters, photographers, and filmmakers, it produced still photographs and motion pictures of the test operations at Wright Field, as well as training films for the Army Air Corps. After World War II, translators working in the library translated over 55,000 captured documents detailing Nazi Germany's aeronautical research and development programs. (AFLCMC.)

In 1917, a young woman named Sarah Clark applied for a civil service position at McCook Field. Hired as a "production expert," she became chief of Central Files nine months later. Her first task was reorganizing the entire file library using the Dewey decimal system. In 1927, Central Files moved to Wright Field, where Clark supervised a staff of analysts and clerks who collected and preserved the records of all flight research, testing, and development performed at McCook Field, Wright Field (below, around 1936), and Wright-Patterson Air Force Base. By the 1950s, Clark was supervising 63,000 cubic feet of files. In 1955, the Air Force decided to send its old files to the National Archives for preservation. Clark personally supervised the packing of over 40 years of files, making sure each was carefully boxed with a detailed inventory list; then, she retired. Today, the US Air Force's Research and Development Case Files are known as the Sarah Clark Collection. Historians treasure this collection, which traces the entire history of American aviation from World War I to the jet age. (Left, illustration by Jill Josupeit; both, AFLCMC.)

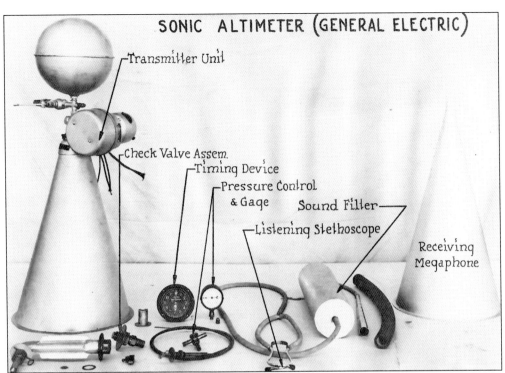

SONIC ALTIMETER (GENERAL ELECTRIC)

Transmitter Unit

Check Valve Assem.

Timing Device

Pressure Control & Gage

Sound Filter

Listening Stethoscope

Receiving Megaphone

The General Electric sonic altimeter was developed in 1931 by the US Army Air Service. It emitted a series of high-pitched sounds, like those made by a bat, which would bounce off the ground then back to the aircraft to be converted into a measurement in feet. In testing, the sonic altimeter was found to be more accurate in rain or fog than the air pressure altimeter but was never put into production. This photograph was taken by the Equipment Section on September 24, 1931. (NMUSAF.)

In 1931, the Equipment Section and General Electric developed the sonic field beacon, pictured on September 24, 1931. To help pilots land in bad weather or darkness, the beacon emitted a series of short, high-pitched whistles from three megaphones. A beacon would be placed at each end of the field, arranged so that they would sound alternately. When the sound became continuous, a pilot knew he was over the center of the field. (NMUSAF.)

Few staff members at Wright Field have saved more lives than Col. Edward L. Hoffman. From the time of its establishment at McCook Field in 1918, the Army's Parachute Board was headed by Hoffman. Initially, the board's team included Floyd Smith, Guy M. Ball, James M. Russell, and James J. Higgins. They were given the task of developing a parachute that was not attached to the airplane, as had been the case in World War I, but that would allow the pilot to escape and then release the parachute once the he was safely away from the plane. It had to withstand the shock of opening, even at high speed, and be simple to pack and maintain. In 1919, the team selected Smith's Model A parachute for the first live tests. A modified version of the Model A went into production in 1922. In 1927, the Parachute Board moved to Wright Field, where it became the Parachute and Clothing Branch. At Wright Field, Hoffman developed the Hoffman Triangle Parachute, a parachute that could be guided during descent. His work with larger parachutes led to the development of parachutes that could slow the descent of a large bomb. These were employed on nuclear weapons and, later, on space capsules. By World War II, even larger parachutes were being developed at Wright Field that could safely lower an entire airplane. Hoffman is seen wearing his Hoffman Triangle Parachute in this 1931 photograph. (AFLCMC.)

The world's first free-fall parachute, the Model A, is displayed by its inventor, Floyd Smith, in this 1919 photograph. It was successfully drop-tested at McCook Field 11 times using dummies before the first free-fall parachute jump was made by team member Leslie Irvin on April 28, 1919. Because of this test, the Model A is sometimes erroneously called the Irvin Parachute. The backpack design was not put into production, because it would not fit in a cockpit. (AFLCMC.)

Because the backpack parachute would not fit in a cockpit, the Parachute Board moved the pack to the bottom seat cushion. Board member Guy M. Ball models the new design, which was first used by McCook Field test pilot Harold R. Harris on October 20, 1922, to escape a crashing Loening monoplane. Used throughout World War II, the seat-pack parachute was standard issue to American pilots until the introduction of ejection seats in the late 1940s. (AFLCMC.)

Development of observation aircraft at Wright Field began with the testing of the Thomas-Morse XO-19. On June 16, 1928, Thomas-Morse received a contract for four all-metal, air-cooled observation biplanes. Powered by a Pratt & Whitney R-1340-3, the first XO-19 arrived at Wright Field in the spring of 1929. Constructed of riveted dural tubing, with corrugated dural covering the fuselage and control surfaces, it was the first all-metal observation plane to enter service. By the time production started in late 1929, the company had already been bought by Consolidated Aircraft. (AFLCMC.)

Douglas had been the principal supplier of observation aircraft to the US Army and attempted to regain that position with the XO-31, which arrived at Wright Field in early 1931. Like the Thomas-Morse O-19, the XO-31 featured a corrugated dural-covered fuselage, though with a single fabric-covered gull wing. The prototype remained at Wright Field for some time while engineers tried to fix a variety of stability issues. Never put into production, the O-31 led to the development of the O-43, a redesign which saw limited production. (AFLCMC.)

A Douglas O-25A is pictured while undergoing testing at Wright Field on May 20, 1933. The Wright Field spearhead is clearly visible below the cockpit. The O-25 was an upgrade of the Douglas O-2H, powered by a 600-horsepower Curtiss Conqueror V-1570 engine in place of the O-2's 400-horsepower Liberty engine. By the time this photograph was taken, the O-25A had been in service for three years. This aircraft was likely being used to test new equipment. (AFLCMC.)

The Curtiss O-39 Falcon was an O-1G refitted with a Conqueror engine. The staff of the Fairfield Air Depot (FAD) added a rear cockpit enclosure to the prototype while it was being tested at Patterson Field. The canopy was later incorporated into the 10 production O-39s. Not all modifications made at Wright Field were made by Wright engineers. This is an example of the staff of the FAD making a modification that later became part of the final design. (AFLCMC.)

In February 1930, a board of officers from Wright Field's Materiel Division recommended the acquisition of an aircraft specifically for aerial photography. It needed to have "good stability directionally, longitudinally, and laterally" and be "controllable at all speeds [with] good visibility, and ample cabin space for camera installation and operation" while operating at 16,000 feet. Twelve aircraft underwent extensive evaluations at Wright Field before the Fairchild 71 was selected. Fifteen were built under the new designation F-1A and, later, C-8A. The rugged and dependable F-1A was the first official Air Corps photographic aircraft. For the next 10 years, it remained the Army's sole photographic aircraft type. (AFLCMC.)

When Wright Field opened in 1927, the Army's standard transport was the Atlantic C-2 Bird of Paradise, an American-built military version of the Dutch-made Fokker F.IX. Three C-2s (like the one pictured) and eight slightly larger C-2As were in use by 1928. In 1930, the staff of the Materiel Division wanted to replace them with a single-engine transport that could be operated more economically. Offers were made to aircraft manufacturers for test aircraft, although few single-engine transports were in production at the time. (AFLCMC.)

Although the contract requested a single-engine design, most of the aircraft submitted for evaluation had two or three engines. Among the entries was the Ford 4-AT-A Trimotor, which had been in production since 1926. While the C-2 had a wooden wing, the Ford Trimotor was all metal, and had a reputation for ruggedness and reliability. Although it did not meet contract specifications, a total of 13 were purchased by the Air Corps as C-3A, C-4, and C-4A transports. Pictured is the first C-4A, which arrived at Wright Field on January 9, 1931. (AFLCMC.)

TYPE	ENGINE	CEILING	HIGH SPEED	CAPACITY
EXPERIMENTAL	575 HP	NOT OBTAINED	143.7 MPH	8 PASSENGERS
TRANSPORT				
YIC27 BELLANCA				

Perhaps the most unique entry in the competition was the Bellanca Y1C-27 Airbus. Better known as the "Flying W", the Airbus was unusual because its external wing bracing, landing gear, and fuselage were all utilized as lifting surfaces. The Y1C-27 did surprisingly well in tests at Wright Field and fulfilled most of the contract requirements. Fourteen were acquired as the C-27, which offered better performance and could carry more cargo than the Ford C-4 and Fokker C-14 transports. The C-27 performed excellently, remaining in service until the late 1930s, when it was replaced by the C-47. (AFLCMC.)

After skipping the designation C-13 for superstitious reasons, in 1931, the Army purchased 20 Fokker F.XIV under the designation Y1C-14. Powered by a single Wright 1750-3 Hornet engine, the C-14 featured a parasol wing with a 59-foot span. The pilot sat in an open cockpit, which could accommodate up to six passengers, about 30 feet down the fuselage. Underpowered, the C-14 is perhaps best remembered as the first Air Corps airplane to receive the "A" (C-14A) designation following an engine upgrade, instead of a new number (a system that continues to this day). The sole C-14B (s/n 31-381) was used extensively at Wright Field for testing parachutes and navigation aids. On August 23, 1937, it made the world's first automated landing at Patterson Field. Three senior project engineers from Wright Field were onboard as observers—Capt. Carl Crane, director of the Instrument and Navigation Laboratory; Capt. George Holloman, assistant director; and Raymond Stout, project engineer. The historic landing followed two years of preparation and occurred just a few hundred feet from the Huffman Flying Field, where on December 31, 1913, Orville Wright had made the world's first flight using an autopilot. (AFLCMC.)

CURTISS YC - 30 WRIGHT GIR-1820-23 ENGINE.

In 1933, two very unusual airplanes arrived at Wright Field for testing. Not part of the transport aircraft competition, the two Curtiss YC-30 Condors (one is pictured here at Wright Field in 1933) had been ordered for a very special purpose. A modified version of the Curtiss Condor airliner, the YC-30 featured many luxury innovations not found on normal airliners. The fabric-covered fuselage was lined with sound-absorbing material, making it extremely quiet. Each passenger seat had its own controls for hot and cold air, and the lavatory featured hot and cold running water. Following evaluations at Wright Field, both were redesignated C-30 Condors and delivered to Bolling Field in Washington, DC, where they were used to transport high-ranking government officials and visiting dignitaries. The C-30s paved the way for future military VIP aircraft that would later carry the designation VC-, such as the VC-25, better known as Air Force One. By 1935, both C-30s had been replaced by newer executive transports. Stripped of their amenities, they were used for airmail service before ending up as maintenance trainers in late 1937. Both were stricken from Air Corps service in 1938, one in June and the other in September. (AFLCMC.)

In the 1920s and early 1930s, the Army was responsible for coastal defense. In the early 1930s, two amphibious transports were tested at Wright Field. The Sikorsky XC-6 (above) was the Army's first amphibious cargo plane. Based on the Sikorsky S-38B, the XC-6 was tested at Wright Field in 1930. After acceptance, it was sent to Bolling Field in Washington, DC, as a staff transport. Later, 10 C-6As were purchased with upgraded R-1340 Wasp engines. Used for coastal patrol, they had a top speed of only 125 miles per hour. All were grounded and scrapped in the summer of 1933. The Douglas Y1C-21 Dolphin (below) incorporated a more modern design. Evaluated in 1931, it was a high-wing monoplane with room for six passengers. In 1933, the Air Corps's fleet of C-21s were redesignated as OA-3s (observation amphibian). They became the Air Corps' s first effective amphibious aircraft and were used to develop many of the air-sea search-and-rescue techniques employed in World War II. (Both, AFLCMC.)

Among the least-known of Army Air Corps aircraft were the autogyros. In 1935, the Materiel Division recognized a need for autogyros for observation, reconnaissance, and artillery spotting. A competition was held in 1936 at Wright Field between aircraft from the Kellett Autogyro Corporation and the Pitcairn Autogyro Company. Kellett offered its KD-1 Autogyro (above), which was designated YG-1. The YG-1 was 28 feet long, with rotors 60 feet in diameter. Powered by a 225-horsepower Jacobs L-4 radial engine, it featured a wing pylon in front of the cockpit for easy access. The Pitcairn YG-2 (below) was 23 feet long with rotors 30 feet in diameter and was powered by a 400-horsepower Wright R-975-E engine. Both featured tandem open cockpits. Following flight tests, the Kellett design was selected. Sixteen were eventually purchased in several configurations as observation aircraft. In 1941, the "G" designation for "Gyrocopter" was changed to "R" for "Rotary Wing." Though the "R" designation is usually associated with Army helicopters, it originated with gyrocopters. (Both, AFLCMC.)

In 1937, work at Wright Field showed that it should be possible to produce a fast attack bomber capable of carrying 1,200 pounds of bombs for 1,200 miles at a speed of 200 miles per hour. The competition that followed produced many legendary aircraft. Bell, Douglas, North American, Martin, and Stearman all participated, though Bell soon abandoned its design. Martin offered its Model 167, which arrived at Wright Field in March 1939. Designated the XA-22, it featured a slender, tapering body. With a crew of three, it could reach 280 miles per hour, making it the fastest entry. The Army passed on it, but France ordered 115, which went to England when France fell in 1940. Named the Martin Maryland, 450 were used by the Royal Air Force during World War II. (AFLCMC.)

North American's offering was the NA-40. Developed from the XB-21 bomber, the smaller NA-40 featured tricycle landing gear. Initial performance figures were disappointing, so the prototype's Pratt & Whitney R-1830 engines were replaced with more powerful Wright R-2600s, creating the NA-40B. The NA-40B was lost in an accident at Wright Field on April 11, 1939, but the Army was not yet through with it. In late 1939, it was put into production as a medium bomber, the famous B-25 Mitchell. By the time production ended, 9,816 B-25s had been produced. The US Air Force retired its last B-25 in May 1960, though many still fly as vintage warbirds. (AFLCMC.)

Douglas offered its Model 7B. Powered by two 1,100-horsepower Pratt & Whitney R-2830 Double Wasp engines, the Model 7B was fast and maneuverable. Following testing at Wright Field, the aircraft was the favored entry in the competition. Unfortunately, during a demonstration to the French government, it was lost in a crash in Los Angeles, California, on January 23, 1939, ending its chances for a contract. Foreign orders saved it, and it eventually entered American service as the A-20 Havoc. By the time production ended on September 20, 1944, 7,478 A-20 Havocs and P-70 Nighthawks had been built. (AFLCMC.)

Though the competition produced many legendary aircraft, the Stearman entry was not one of them. Stearman's X-100 was powered by two 1,400-horsepower Pratt & Whitney R-2180-7 radial engines and could reach 257 miles per hour. It could carry 2,700 pounds of bombs and had nine defensive machine guns, but its most distinctive characteristic was its large canopy, which resembled those found on German aircraft. Following the loss of the Douglas and North American planes, the Army purchased the sole X-100, renaming it the XA-21 (s/n 40-191)—but only after it received a more traditional canopy. By the time the plane returned to Wright Field for further testing, the Stearman Aircraft Corporation had been bought by Boeing, who abandoned the project. (AFLCMC.)

As aircraft became more powerful, the Air Corps needed better primary trainers. A circular proposal in 1935 produced a bid from Stearman for its Model 75, which became the PT-13 Kaydet, powered by a 220-horsepower Lycoming R-680 radial engine. Stearman's initial contract was for 25 PT-13s, with delivery beginning in March 1936. Thousands of Army and Navy pilots would earn their wings flying Stearmans, among the most important trainers in history. Engine changes resulted in the PT-17, PT-18, and PT-27. By the time production ended in 1944, over 10,000 had been manufactured, including 2,100 PT-13s for the Army Air Forces, making it the most-produced biplane in history. (AFLCMC.)

Believing that a monoplane would exhibit flight characteristics more similar to a modern combat plane, the Air Corps issued a circular for a monoplane trainer in 1939. Eighteen designs were evaluated, with the Fairchild M-62 being declared the winner. Fairchild received an initial contract for 275 PT-19 Cornell trainers on September 22, 1939. By the time production ended, nearly 6,400 PT-19, PT-23, and PT-26 Cornell trainers had been built, for use in 21 countries. Thousands of American pilots received their first flights in Cornells before moving on to the more difficult Stearman. (AFLCMC.)

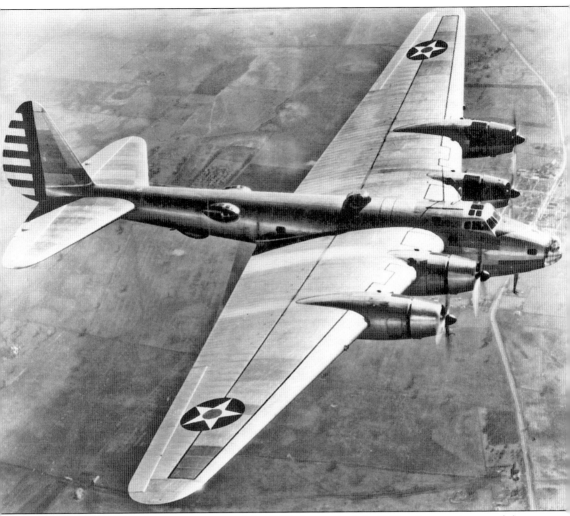

The second epic bomber competition of the 1930s began in July 1933, when engineers of the Materiel Division determined that engines now existed of sufficient power to produce a heavy bomber capable of carrying 2,000 pounds of bombs a distance of 5,000 miles at a speed of 200 miles per hour. The proposal was known as Project A and resulted in the Boeing Model 294, which the Air Corps designated XB-15. The XB-15 was to be powered by four 2,600-horsepower Allison V-3420 liquid-cooled engines, but production problems forced a switch to Pratt & Whitney R-1830 engines of only 850 horsepower. Like the Barling Bomber of the 1920s, the XB-15 was severely underpowered, capable of only 145 miles per hour when fully loaded. Following testing at Wright Field, it set several records for lifting cargo, once carrying 22,046 pounds to an altitude of 8,228 feet. On May 6, 1943, it was redesignated the XC-105, although its devoted crew had already named it "Grandpappy." Following conversion to a cargo plane, it was assigned to Albrook Field in Panama. In June 1945, "Grandpappy" was ordered to be pushed into a swamp in Panama, where it remains to this day. (AFLCMC.)

The XB-15 proved that very large bombers were impractical, so in 1935, the Materiel Division issued Army Circular Proposal 35-356, calling for a multiengine bomber capable of carrying 2,000 pounds of bombs for 2,000 miles at 200 miles per hour. Martin, Douglas, and Boeing all submitted designs. Martin offered the Model 146 (above). An updated version of its popular B-10, it featured a wider fuselage with room for two pilots seated side by side. It was little better than the earlier B-10. Douglas's entry was the DB-1 (below, in Wright Field markings). The DB-1 was basically a DC-2 airliner with a slightly longer wingspan and a deeper fuselage to accommodate bomb loads. The DB-1 was actually inferior to the earlier B-10 in many ways. Neither was what the Air Corps was looking for. (Both, NMUSAF.)

Taking advantage of the ambiguous term "multiengine," Boeing's entry would become one of the most important aircraft ever tested at Wright Field, the four-engine Model 299. Boeing's experience in building the XB-15 was put to use to produce a scaled-down version that fit the Air Corps's requirements perfectly. The Model 299 could carry up to 4,800 pounds of bombs on two internal racks and was initially protected by five machine guns. A reporter for the *Seattle Times* named it the "Flying Fortress," and Boeing soon trademarked the title. On August 20, 1935, the Model 299 flew from Boeing's factory in Seattle to Wright Field in nine hours and three minutes at an average speed of 252 miles per hour, far exceeding the capabilities of the Martin and Douglas aircraft. The procurement staff at Wright Field were quick to recognize the significance of the Flying Fortress as a strategic weapon capable of inflicting devastating damage if produced in sufficient numbers. Before the competition was over, Maj. Gen. Frank Andrews suggested ordering 65 Flying Fortresses. The Model 299 won the competition easily. (NMUSAF.)

All looked promising for the Boeing Model 299 until October 30, 1935. On an evaluation flight, tragedy struck when the sleek bomber rose from Wright Field, stalled, and crashed to the ground near the present location of the Air Force Museum. Onboard were pilot Maj. Ployer P. "Pete" Hill, chief of the Flight Testing Section at Wright Field, and copilot Lt. Donald Putt, the project pilot. Behind them was Leslie Tower, Boeing's chief test pilot and the first man to fly the Model 299. Also aboard were Henry Igo of Pratt & Whitney and C.B. Benton of Boeing. While Putt and Igo staggered from the burning wreckage, spectators Lt. Robert K. Giovannoli and Lt. Leonard F. "Jake" Harmon climbed onto the burning aircraft. Giovannoli pulled Tower through the copilot's window, but Hill was trapped, his foot caught under the rudder pedal. Using a penknife, the pair cut his shoe off and pulled him through the window, then, badly burned, they exited the aircraft. The cause of the crash was determined to be a failure to disengage the plane's gust locks, a mechanism that locks the flight control surfaces while the plane is on the ground. A small handle had not been pulled back. Ironically, the gust locks had been added as a safety feature. Hill never regained consciousness and died later that day. Tower, according to one historian, "blamed himself for the accident and (although not seriously injured) died a few days later because he no longer wanted to live." With the Model 299 out of the competition, the inferior B-18 was ordered into production. (AFLCMC.)

Believing the Model 299 was too complicated, Congress threatened to halt further funding. To avoid future accidents like the one at Wright Field, the Air Corps developed a preflight checklist for the Model 299. The checklist was so successful it was soon applied to all Air Corps aircraft. Now required by the Federal Aviation Administration, the preflight checklist has become a standard procedure, performed thousands of times a day at the start of every flight. ((AFLCMC.)

The "exceedingly interesting possibilities" created by the Boeing bomber prompted the Air Corps to find a legal loophole, and 13 new airplanes were ordered for evaluation under the designation Y1B-17 on January 17, 1936. More were ordered in 1938 and 1939 as B-17As, and in July 1940, the first large order for 512 B-17Bs was placed, though less than 200 were in service when Pearl Harbor was attacked. In this photograph, a B-17C is seen flying above Wright Field in the early 1940s. (AFLCMC.)

In the summer of 1936, the Air Corps purchased a single, heavily modified Lockheed Model 10-A Electra to use in high-altitude research and pressurization tests. Designated the XC-35 (s/n 36-393), the aircraft was equipped with the world's first functional pressurized cabin, which was designed by Maj. Carl Greene and John Younger of Wright Field's Engineering Division. To withstand stress, the fuselage was redesigned with a near-circular cross section, while the windows were reduced to small slits. The crew consisted of a pilot, copilot, and engineer who controlled the cabin's pressure (below). Produced at a cost of $112,197, the XC-35 was delivered in May 1937 to Wright Field, where it was tested extensively at altitudes up to 30,000 feet, winning the 1937 Collier Trophy for the most significant aircraft development of the year. (Both, NMUSAF.)

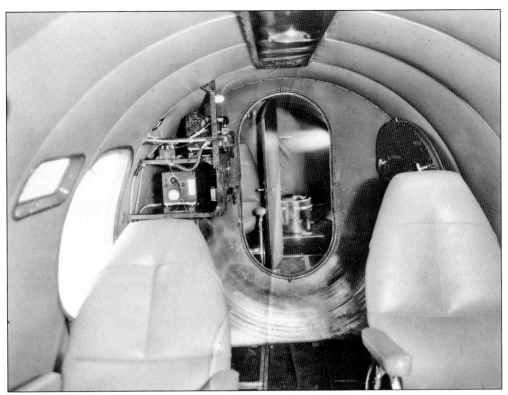

To better withstand stress, the interior was split into two sections separated by a hemispherical steel bulkhead (above). The forward section was pressurized and contained the crew of three, with room for two passengers. Behind the bulkhead was an unpressurized section containing one seat and a rear toilet (right), which was to remain unoccupied at altitudes above 12,000 feet. Knowledge gained from the XC-35 was applied to the Boeing B-29 Superfortress, as well as commercial airliners. In 1948, the XC-35 was donated to the Smithsonian Institution, where it remains in long-term storage. (Both, NMUSAF.)

On August 2, 1939, the Army Air Corps celebrated its 30th anniversary. The date commemorated the day the Army bought its first airplane from the Wright brothers in 1909. Air shows were held at airfields around the country, with the biggest show at Wright Field. The event was hosted by Gen. George H. Brett, chief of the Materiel Division. Invitations were distributed through the press to residents of Dayton and the surrounding areas. In total, 48,600 people attended, traveling by automobile, bus, air, on foot, and on an army of bicycles, while an estimated 25,000 more watched outside. Around 50 aircraft were displayed on the ramp, with platforms set up so that visitors could enter the larger aircraft. The Army Aeronautical Museum in Building 12 was open to the public, and food and beverages were served throughout the day. As an Army band from the V Corps at Fort Hayes in Columbus played, three men from Wright Field manned the loudspeaker and entertained the crowd with their wit. At 3:00 p.m., a cannon signaled the close of the nation's largest pre–World War II military air show. The aircraft at center is a Curtiss YP-37, a P-36 powered by a liquid-cooled Allison V-1710 inline engine producing 1,150 horsepower. Tested in June 1939, the YP-37 led to the development of the more powerful Curtiss P-40 Tomahawk. The bomber in the rear is a Douglas B-18A Bolo. (AFLCMC.)

At 11:00 a.m., Pres. Franklin D. Roosevelt read a prepared speech over the radio as formations of pursuit planes took off to mark the official opening of the ceremony (above). Meanwhile, a luncheon, hosted by Maj. Gen. Henry "Hap" Arnold, was held for 410 visiting aviation dignitaries. Those in attendance included Brig. Gen. William E. Gillmore; Col. F.E. Humphries and Col. Frank P. Lamb, the first and second officers to solo in a military airplane; C.F. Horner, president of the National Aeronautic Association; Robert Hinckley of the Civil Aeronautics Authority; and Dr. George Lewis, director of the National Advisory Committee for Aeronautics. Afterward, all were given a private tour of the base's various laboratories. (Both, AFLCMC.)

By the late 1930s, it was apparent to the staff of the Power Plant Branch that Building 18 lacked enough space to perform long-term durability tests and was ill-suited for testing "foreign object damage." So, the so-called Rabbit Patch was constructed in a remote wooded area on the southern end of Wright Field, near the current I-675 gate. The Rabbit Patch consisted of seven concrete pads with control rooms, where engines could run 24 hours a day, seven days a week, without disturbing anyone. During World War II, the facility provided a vital role in testing wartime engines like the Allison V-1710 pictured above and, later, the first jet engines. The construction of the Page Manor housing complex in 1953 forced the closing of the Rabbit Patch, due to the excessive noise it produced. However, its historic role in aircraft engine development remains. (Both, AFLCMC.)

Four

1940–1948
I WANT AIRPLANES—NOW—
AND LOTS OF THEM

Every military airfield in America was impacted in some way by World War II, but none experienced more growth and activity than Wright Field. In September 1938, Pres. Franklin D. Roosevelt called a meeting of his top military advisers. Hitler's growing military power made it clear that America urgently needed to increase its airpower. "I want airplanes—now—and lots of them," Roosevelt demanded. During the 1930s, the Air Corps had been acquiring about 200 airplanes a year. Suddenly, the goal was 5,500 aircraft in inventory by July 1, 1941. In 1940, Roosevelt increased this to 50,000 airplanes a year, equivalent to the total number of aircraft the military had purchased from 1909 to 1940.

To achieve the president's goals, Wright Field underwent a massive expansion program. In 1941, there were only 40 buildings at Wright Field. By 1944, there were over 300. To maximize use, Wright Field began operating three shifts, around the clock. In December 1939, the staff size at Wright Field was approximately 3,700. By 1944, it had grown to over 50,000, with a payroll of $13.5 million—35 percent of Dayton's total industrial payroll.

To expedite the development of new aircraft, the traditional method of testing competing prototypes was abandoned. By the time the United States entered World War II, manufacturers could no longer afford to divert precious resources and manpower to expensive prototypes. Instead, new aircraft were ordered into production straight off the drawing board, as Wright Field staff tested and refined aircraft that would soon enter production. Wright Field engineers were also responsible for modifying existing aircraft to accommodate new engines, weapons, and equipment as they became available, including modifications for carrying atomic bombs. By the time Japan surrendered in 1945, there were over 800 major—and thousands of minor—programs in development at Wright Field.

In order to test the Air Corps's new generation of heavy bombers, the addition of two reenforced concrete runways was given the highest priority. Taken in 1943, the photograph above shows the 5,569.3-foot-long northwest-southeast Runway 16/34. It was completed in February 1942, just in time to test the Boeing XB-29 Superfortress. Runway 09/27 was longer, at 7,147.7 feet, and ran east-west to take advantage of prevailing winds. In November 1943, a third 6,478.5-foot northeast-southwest runway was added, completing the triangle (below). Wright Field was the first military installation equipped with concrete runways. Closed to jet traffic in 1958, two of Wright Field's original runways were removed when flight operations stopped in 1976. Today, only Runway 09/27 remains, used occasionally by the National Museum of the US Air Force. (Both, AFLCMC.)

During runway construction, captured intelligence reports indicated that the Germans were planning to build inclined runways along the northern coast of France to shorten takeoff distances. The Materiel Division quickly decided to build an inclined runway at Wright Field to test the concept. The Price Brothers Company's contract was modified to include an additional runway with a 10 percent grade to be built on a hillside just east of the hangar complex. Tests with heavy bombers, like the B-50 (above), soon found the accelerated runway was impractical, and it was abandoned. After World War II, it gained a new purpose as one of the top soapbox derby racetracks in the United States (below). Since 1976, it has been the only runway at Wright Field still used regularly, although not for aircraft. (Both, AFLCMC.)

Located within the 4,500 acres donated to the federal government was Tate Hill, one of the highest points in Greene County. The hill had a long history in the area, with Samuel Tate placing a still there in 1816. In 1924, the hill was set aside for a memorial to honor the Wright brothers. Work on the memorial began in early 1940, supported by the Wilbur and Orville Wright Memorial Commission, the Miami Conservancy District, the National Park Service, and the Civilian Conservation Corps. The monument was designed and constructed by Olmsted Brothers. Renamed Wright Brothers Hill, the knoll features an obelisk carved from pink granite mined in North Carolina. The monument was dedicated on August 19, 1940, Orville's 69th birthday. Orville and several of the 119 students he taught to fly at the Huffman Prairie were present for the ceremony. At left, Orville (left) is seen chatting with Maj. Gen. Henry "Hap" Arnold (right) during the dedication ceremony pictured at left. Below, Air Force personnel place wreaths on the memorial every December 17, in commemoration of the first flight. (Both, AFLCMC.)

Igor Sikorsky (left) is seen standing next to Orville Wright at a ceremony on May 17, 1942, marking the first helicopter delivered to the US military. The Sikorsky XR-4 (s/n 41-18874) had flown from the factory in Stratford, Connecticut, to Wright Field—a distance of 761 miles. Because of fuel and weight restrictions, test pilot Charles Lester "Les" Morris had to make the trip in 16 separate flights, for a total flight time of 16 hours and 10 minutes, with Sikorsky joining him for the final leg. Upon arrival, Morris hovered straight up the base's Administration Building before landing, when he and Sikorsky were met by Wright. The aircraft remained at Wright Field, where it was used for flight-testing. Helicopters were not new to Dayton. The Army's first experimental helicopter, the de Bothezat Octopus, was built and tested at McCook Field in 1922. Today, the Sikorsky XR-4 is on display at the National Air and Space Museum's Steven F. Udvar-Hazy Center at Washington Dulles International Airport in Chantilly, Virginia. (AFLCMC.)

On October 12, 1940, Pres. Franklin D. Roosevelt took a motorized tour of Wright Field. Traveling in a motorcade on his way to give a speech in downtown Dayton, the president (below, left in backseat) was accompanied by Orville Wright (seated beside him), former Ohio governor James M. Cox (seated next to Orville), and Maj. Gen. George H. Brett, chief of the Materiel Division, (in front of the president). The visit was more than ceremonial. Wright Field was crucial to Roosevelt's plan for an air force of 50,000 planes a year, and he wanted to inspect the facilities personally. The flagpole (above) is the same one Orville used at the base's dedication in 1927. (Both, AFLCMC.)

The Wright Field staff set up several displays along the president's route through the base, including a demonstration of parachutes (above) and a fatigue test of a Bell P-39 Airacobra (below). After touring Wright Field, the president's motorcade traveled into downtown Dayton, where he gave a speech in Courthouse Square to an estimated 100,000 spectators. (Both, NMUSAF.)

In this view looking northeast in May 1943, the flight line is visible from the new control tower on top of Building 8. When Building 8 opened in early 1943, the Operations Center, which had been located in Hangar 3 since 1929, relocated to Building 8's lower levels. The Operations Center and control tower remained in use until 1976, when all flight operations ceased in Area B. (AFLCMC.)

When finished in 1943, Hangars 1 and 9 were the largest hangars on the field, built for aircraft modification and flight-testing. During World War II, work performed in Hangars 1 and 9 was among the most important and classified at Wright Field. In early 1944, the 59th Boeing B-29 (s/n 42-6259) was moved into Hangar 1, where its bomb bay was secretly modified to accommodate the atomic bomb. Known as Operation Silverplate, the modification was later made to other B-29s, including *Enola Gay* and *Bockscar*, which dropped the atomic bombs on Japan. In 1977, the buildings became the Air Force Museum Annex. Used to store aircraft too large for the museum but too fragile to keep outside, in the 1990s they became the museum's Presidential and Research and Development Galleries, closing on October 1, 2015, when the aircraft were relocated to the museum's new hangar. (AFLCMC.)

Completed in 1944, Hangar 4 consists of five connected bays (4A-E) located along Runway 16/34. It was built to accommodate a growing need for more aircraft modification space, particularly for work on captured enemy aircraft, and much of the work performed here remains classified. On September 9, 1944, Hangar 4E became home to the newly formed Air Force Test Pilot School, which remained there until its move to Edwards Air Force Base on February 4, 1951. The Air Force Orientation Group occupied the buildings during the 1960s and 1970s. In 1977, Hangar 4C-E became the Air Force Museum's Restoration and Storage Facility. (AFLCMC.)

On March 6, 1945, a Lockheed C-60 veered off Runway 16/34 during takeoff and crashed into Hangar 4A, killing the crew of five and three people in the hangar and seriously injuring four others. Eight aircraft were destroyed, including a B-29 and a B-32. The C-60 was carrying a load of parachute-equipped dummies for a drop test. (AFLCMC.)

The sole Douglas XB-19 Hemisphere Defender bomber is pictured making a low pass over Springfield Street near the entrance to Wright Field in late 1942. Designed out of fear that England would fall and the Air Corps would have to strike Germany from bases in the United States, the XB-19 was developed as a successor to the B-17 Flying Fortress. The giant bomber had a wingspan of 212 feet and was 132 feet and two inches long. Its gross weight was more than 140,000 pounds, and it could carry 16,000 pounds of bombs internally and another 20,000 pounds on external racks. The crew of 11 was defended by 12 guns, including two 37-millimeter cannons. Unfortunately, the plane's maximum speed of 212 miles per hour would have made it easy prey for enemy fighters. The bomber was a frequent sight at Wright Field in 1942 and 1943 as the Air Corps tried to fix its problems, but a final analysis concluded that the XB-19, "like the B-15, served only to test, and thus to advance, the engineering knowledge that went into the construction of other and more successful planes." It was scrapped in 1949, though one of its huge tires is on display at the Air Force Museum. (AFLCMC.)

Perhaps the most important aircraft developed at Wright Field during World War II was the Boeing B-29 Superfortress. The XB-29 became one of the field's largest projects, eventually involving virtually every research department and laboratory. The project officer for the XB-29 program was Capt. Donald L. Putt, Materiel Command aeronautical engineer and the test pilot who survived the horrific crash of the Boeing Model 299 in 1935. Development of the XB-29 originated at Wright Field on September 6, 1940, when a contract was issued to Boeing and Consolidated Aircraft for a prototype "super bomber" capable of delivering 20,000 pounds of bombs to a target 2,667 miles away at a speed of 400 miles per hour. The XB-29 combined many Wright Field innovations, including pressurized cabins and radar-controlled guns. The first XB-29 (s/n 41-002) is seen undergoing testing at Wright Field (above). *Bockscar*, the B-29 that dropped the atomic bomb on Nagasaki, is currently on display in the National Museum of the US Air Force (below). (Both, NMUSAF.)

With the dramatic increase in projects and programs brought about by World War II, Wright Field's staff quickly outgrew the base housing. By 1941, base personnel were housed in spare bedrooms around Dayton, as families traded a son who had gone off to fight for an airman stationed at the base. Frequent requests for new housing were not met until 1943, when the Army Air Forces began construction of Wood City and Skyway Park. By 1944, the staff had grown to over 50,000 and the entire hilltop area had been acquired. What had formerly been farmland was transformed into additional laboratories and barracks. Taken in 1944, this photograph shows the area along Skyline Drive and Springfield Street. The Wright Brothers Memorial is at far right. Near the center is a fenced-in area that served as a prisoner-of-war camp for German and Italian prisoners during World War II. (AFLCMC.)

The key to solving the housing shortage was the construction of Skyway Park (area on left), a 190-acre housing complex at the intersection of present-day Kauffman Avenue and Colonel Glenn Highway. When completed in the summer of 1944, Skyway Park contained 546 single-family housing units for civilian engineers and technicians working in the laboratories at Wright Field, as well as five Skyway Lodge dormitories that housed 640 women, with its own clinic and cafeteria. On October 25, 1947, it was officially transferred from the National Housing Agency to the Army Air Forces and became Area D. Skyway Park closed in 1957, and many of the buildings were sold and moved off-base, while the rest were demolished. In 1963, the land was transferred to the State of Ohio. Some of the site now lies under the McClerron Memorial Skyway, while the rest is part of Wright State University. (AFLCMC.)

Buildings 24–26 (above) are seen under construction in late 1941. Collectively, they formed Wright Field's wind tunnel complex. Completed in 1942, Building 24 contained the enormous Massie Memorial Wind Tunnel, a 20-foot-diameter test chamber capable of assessing very large models at airspeeds up to 400 miles per hour. Its two 16-bladed fans were driven by a single 40,000-horsepower electric motor (left, during installation). Building 24A was the power building, and 24B was the test chamber. Building 25 was added in 1944 and housed a 10-foot, a two-foot, and a six-inch supersonic wind tunnel. Dr. Bernhard Goerthert, the German transonic pioneer who came to Wright Field under Operation Paperclip, performed groundbreaking supersonic research here. Collectively, this complex was known as "Hurricane Hill." (Both, AFLCMC.)

The size of the 20-foot wind tunnel is demonstrated by a group of AAF officers standing inside its throat. Models with wingspans of up to 16 feet were tested here during World War II at speeds up to 400 miles per hour. The tunnel was dismantled in 1960, though Wright-Patterson's two-foot Trisonic Gasdynamic Facility continues to perform tests at subsonic, transonic, and supersonic speeds. (AFLCMC.)

Completed in 1944, Building 27 is the Vertical Wind Tunnel. Originally designed to test aircraft spin characteristics and parachute designs, it can accommodate parachutes up to six feet in diameter. It was used to test parachute drag, opening shock, and retardation stability. In the 1940s and 1950s, free-flight aircraft models were tested to develop ways to recover from tailspins. From the 1950s to 1970s, it was used to test rotary wings, ejection-seat stabilization systems, oil flow models, and force-pressure measurements. Today, it is used to instruct military paratroopers in free-fall techniques. (AFLCMC.)

Brig. Gen. Franklin O. Carroll was chief of the Engineering Division throughout World War II. Known as the "Buck Rogers Division" because of the fantastic designs that were often tested, the division's goal was always to be "three years ahead of the procession" in continuously developing new equipment for the Army Air Forces. By 1943, Carroll was supervising over 800 major research projects in laboratories containing over $50 million worth of equipment. (AFLCMC.)

The Physiological Research Laboratory was established at Wright Field on May 18, 1935. Operated by Army medical officers, its purpose was to study the effects of flight on living beings. Built by Capt. Harry G. Armstrong in 1938, the first human centrifuge in the United States was used to study the effects of g-forces on pilots. Capable of speeds up to 80 revolutions per minute and 20 times the force of gravity, it was replaced in 1965 by the Air Force Research Laboratory's Dynamic Environment Simulator (DES) in Building 33. Regularly used by NASA, the DES operated until February 2, 2007. (AFLCMC.)

The Psychological Research Laboratory designed equipment to measure the effects of speed, altitude, and duration on flight crews, as well as equipment to eliminate their effects. The lab employed three high-altitude pressure chambers; the largest was 31 feet long and eight feet in diameter (pictured above on December 23, 1943, and below in 1937). It could simulate altitudes up to 80,000 feet above sea level, temperatures of -65 degrees Fahrenheit, and a rate of climb of over 600 miles per hour. Telephones allowed test subjects to report their reactions and receive instructions. During World War II, the chambers were instrumental in the development of high-altitude clothing, pressure suits, and breathing apparatuses. (Both, author's collection.)

In 1938, a wheel and tire research facility was established in Building 31. Its purpose was to perform research and development on all landing gear systems and components, including wheels, tires, inner tubes, braking systems, steering devices, and related hardware. Drop-test machines were employed to test entire landing gear assemblies on all types of surfaces (left). Still in use by both military and civilian contractors, Building 31 remains the world's largest landing gear test facility, possessing both the world's largest tire dynamometer and the most powerful drop-test machine. The 192-inch dynamometer (below) can test a tire-wheel-brake assembly at 200 miles per hour under a 290,000-pound load. It was used extensively to test the space shuttle's landing gear. By 1944, Building 31's windows had to be filled in due to the force of bursting tires blowing them all out. (Both, AFLCMC.)

One of the greatest challenges facing Wright Field was noise. When the wind tunnels, torque stands, propeller stands, and the Rabbit Patch were all operating at the same time, the sounds could be heard as far away as Fairfield and Osborn. The arrival of jet engines in the late 1940s only made matters worse. During World War II, many modifications were made in an effort to reduce noise. In 1944, an acoustical enclosure known as Building 20A was built around the propeller test rigs. Its 12-foot thick concrete walls have 19 open side bays containing porous concrete sound baffles designed at Wright Field. The two hexagon cages nearby (below, right) are for testing helicopter rotors. (Both, AFLCMC.)

Building 65, the Static Test Building, is pictured under construction in early 1944 (above) and on October 2, 1944 (below). This massive eight-story Art Deco building was intended for structural testing of the huge Consolidated B-36 Peacemaker bomber, which was too large to be tested in Building 23. The building was constructed in a novel manner. First, two separate three-sided concrete buildings were constructed 180 feet apart (above). Then, steel trusses were placed on top, connecting them. The east side features an enormous six-panel steel hangar door. The Army Air Corps star is still displayed on both the east and west sides of the building today. (Both, AFLCMC.)

The B-36 originated from an Army circular released on April 11, 1941, for an intercontinental bomber capable of reaching Germany from Canada. Fear that the United States might have to bomb Germany from bases in Newfoundland led to a revival of the concept that had spawned the earlier XB-19. On May 3, 1941, Consolidated offered a six-engine design with a range of 10,000 miles and a 10,000-pound bomb load. At 163 feet long, the B-36 was too large to undergo static testing in Building 23, necessitating the construction of Building 65 (above) in early 1944. Static tests required tossing 10-pound bags of lead shot onto the wings while the aircraft hung at different attack angles. Laborers were required to throw the bags 25 feet or higher onto the wing's surfaces. At 132 feet tall, Building 65 was the tallest building at Wright Field until the 148-foot-tall Wright Laser Communications Laboratory, or Building 620 (below), was erected on the hilltop in 1967. (Both, AFLCMC.)

The Thunderstorm Project was the nation's first large-scale scientific study of thunderstorms and was the first meteorological study to employ radar and aircraft. From May to September 1947, a fleet of P-61C Black Widow fighters operated out of the Clinton County Army Air Force Base (now Wilmington Air Park). The area was chosen for its tendency to experience both frontal and non-frontal thunderstorms. Air Materiel Command pilots flew five P-61Cs simultaneously in stacked formation through thunderstorms, collecting data using the planes' SCR-720 radar while a high-powered ground radar located near Jamestown tracked the aircraft. According to Roscoe Braham Jr., senior analyst for the project, "No storm was to be avoided because it appeared too large or violent." The Thunderstorm Project proved that radar could be used to guide an aircraft around a thunderstorm and that aircraft could be employed to study storms, paving the way for the Hurricane Hunters. In January 1948, the P-61Cs were reassigned to Wright Field, where they were employed in the Air Force's first ejection-seat tests. Although only 41 P-61Cs were produced, two survive in museums today because they were flying with the Thunderstorm Project while the other P-61s were being scrapped. (NMUSAF.)

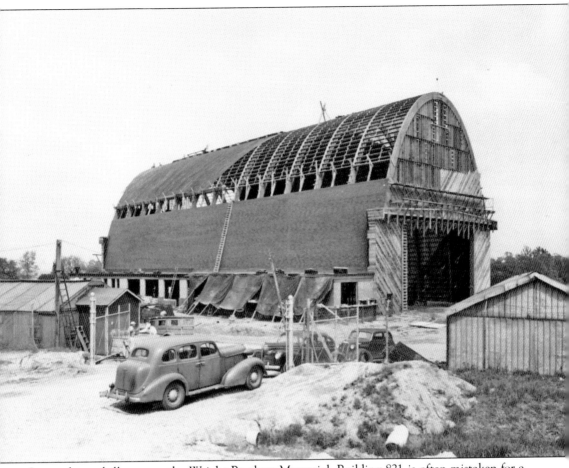

Located on a hilltop near the Wright Brothers Memorial, Building 821 is often mistaken for a blimp hangar. Built in 1948 to test radar equipment, it was constructed entirely of wood (no metal was used). Known as "the Cathedral," or "the Barn," Building 821 is actually the "birthplace of stealth." It was here, in the early 1950s, that William F. Bahret, the so-called Father of Radar Camouflage, performed the world's first experiments on the relationship between shape and radar detection. By the late 1950s, his Propagation Group was developing radar signature enhancements for decoys. In the 1960s, his Signature Technology Office was developing "low observable" designs for airplanes, ships, missiles, and tanks and pioneering the first radar-absorbing coatings for aircraft. Building 821 was one of the most influential laboratories at Wright Field. Research performed there pioneered a revolution in aircraft design. A leaky roof, poor heating, and security concerns ended testing in 1990, and in 1991, the building was reassigned to Logistics Supply as a storage shed, though it remains one of the most historically significant structures in the Air Force inventory. (AFLCMC.)

Howard Hughes was instrumental in developing the Lockheed Constellation for Trans World Airlines (TWA), but the planes were soon needed for World War II. When the second prototype C-69 Constellation (s/n 43-10310) was completed, it was to be flown straight to Wright Field for testing. Hughes had other ideas. With the aircraft painted in TWA markings, Hughes flew it from Burbank, California, to Washington, DC, in a record-breaking six hours and 58 minutes. After gaining the publicity he sought, Hughes personally flew the aircraft to Wright Field, where the TWA markings were washed off. On April 26, 1944, Col. George Hatcher, the C-69 project officer, invited members of the press and Orville Wright to attend a demonstration flight. During the flight, Wright was invited into the cockpit and given the copilot's seat. When Colonel Hatcher got up to allow another pilot to take his seat, he briefly let Wright take the controls. Wright reportedly said, "I let the machine take care of itself. I always said airplanes could fly themselves if you let them alone." It would be his last time piloting an airplane. Following his second heart attack, Orville Wright died on January 30, 1948, and is buried next to Wilbur Wright at Woodland Cemetery in Dayton, Ohio. (AFLCMC.)

Five

Operation LUSTY
LUftwaffe Secret TechnologY

During World War II, the Technical Intelligence School at Wright Field was responsible for training Air Intelligence Teams (AITs), whose job was to recover captured German Luftwaffe equipment for study by the US Army Air Forces. Dispatched to Europe, the AIT teams had to compete with 32 other Allied technical intelligence groups who converged upon German crash sites to collect artifacts and equipment. Material collected by the AIT teams was sent back to Wright Field for testing and study.

By 1944, the intelligence experts at Wright Field had compiled a list of advanced German aircraft technology they wanted located and brought to the United States. Under the leadership of former Wright Field test pilot Col. Harold E. Watson, Watson's "Whizzers" were pilots, engineers, and maintenance men whose job was to locate the equipment on Wright Field's blacklists. The Whizzers were composed of two teams: one collected jet aircraft, while the other collected piston-powered aircraft and non-flyable jet and rocket aircraft.

As hostilities ended, on April 22, 1945, Watson's Whizzers were placed under the command of the Exploitation Division and given the code name Operation LUSTY (LUftwaffe Secret TechnologY). The Whizzers continued to collect enemy aircraft and weapons, while another group examined German production facilities, collected documents, and recruited German scientists. By May 1945, the Whizzers were recruiting German test pilots to help them fly captured aircraft to France for transport to the United States.

The Whizzers traveled by jeep, truck, and occasionally by air to locate the aircraft on Wright Field's blacklists, always trying to stay one step ahead of British and Soviet teams with the same objectives. Once located, the aircraft were flown to Cherbourg, France, where they were cocooned against the saltwater and placed on board the HMS *Reaper*, an escort carrier on loan from the British. Upon arrival in the United States, the captured aircraft were divided between the Army Air Forces and the Navy. Aircraft assigned to the AAF were transported to Wright Field, where they quickly filled Hanger 4's five connected bays. When Wright Field was full, additional aircraft were flown to Freeman Field in Seymour, Indiana. By the time Operation LUSTY ended, its teams had acquired 16,280 items for evaluation, totaling 6,200 tons of material, of which 2,398 items were selected for special investigation.

German aircraft recovered by Operation LUSTY were first shown to the public on Saturday, October 15, 1945, during the AAF Air Fair. The purpose of the fair was to display advances in aviation made during World War II. Over $150 million worth of equipment was shown to the public for the first time and, in an unprecedented move, cameras were welcome. Many aircraft that had been top secret only a week before were suddenly available for the public to see and touch. Both the Heinkel He-162 A-2 Volksjäger (Werknummer 120230) pictured above and the Messerschmitt Me-163 B-1a Komet (Werknummer 191301) seen below were captured by Watson's "Whizzers" and evaluated at Wright Field. Both are now at the Smithsonian Institution in Washington, DC. (Both, AFLCMC.)

The October 1945 AAF Air Fair was only intended to be a weekend event. When over 500,000 people flocked to Wright Field in the first two days, it was extended to a full week. By the time it closed, over a million people from 27 countries had attended, making it the largest event ever held at Wright Field. The Bachman Ba-349 A-1 Natter seen above was captured by advancing US forces in Austria, while the Junkers Ju-388 L-1 (Werknummer 560049) pictured below was captured by Watson's "Whizzers" and flown by Colonel Watson himself. Both are now sole surviving examples and remain in storage at the Smithsonian Institution. (Both, AFLCMC.)

The largest German aircraft ever tested at Wright Field was the huge Junkers Ju-290 A-4 (Werknummer 0165). With a range of over 3,800 miles, the Ju-290 represented the pinnacle of German long-range transport and reconnaissance aircraft. This aircraft was captured when it arrived at Munich-Riem Airport from Czechoslovakia on May 8, 1945, carrying 80 women of the Luftwaffe auxiliary who did not want to fall into Russian hands. On July 28, 1945, Colonel Watson personally flew the Ju-290 from Orly Airport (Paris-Orly) to Wright Field via the Azores. In Europe, Watson named the aircraft *Alles Kaputt* (*All Is Lost*), a phrase he often overheard German soldiers using at the end of the war. The plane was flown frequently at air shows at Wright Field and Freeman Field. Sadly, despite orders from Gen. Henry "Hap" Arnold to preserve one example of each captured aircraft, *Alles Kaputt* was scrapped at Wright Field on December 12, 1946. (AFLCMC.)

Six

ACCIDENTS
YOUTH WAS THE SAVING GRACE

By the end of World War II, there were over 200 different types of aircraft at Wright Field undergoing flight-testing. They included American-made fighters, bombers, transports, trainers, helicopters, reconnaissance aircraft, and liaison aircraft, as well as many foreign-built aircraft being evaluated for US service and a huge collection of captured enemy aircraft. From 1940 to 1945, Wright Field represented a brief, golden moment in history when a military test pilot could be asked to fly anything and everything. Test pilots often flew 100 hours a week or more as they methodically tested the aircraft's capabilities against rigorous standards. Millions of dollars in contracts were on the line, though the safety of the pilots who would soon fly these aircraft into combat was of even greater concern. If the aircraft's performance was off by more than one percent from the promised goal, the contractor faced substantial penalties and even a loss of contract.

World War II provided a wealth of pilots who had distinguished themselves in combat, and it was from these ranks that Wright Field gained its test pilot corps. Each was carefully selected and brought to Wright Field to apply his experience to America's newest combat aircraft and to evaluate the capabilities of the enemy's airplanes. Being asked to join was one of the greatest honors an Army Air Forces pilot could achieve. The job was among the most dangerous in the military. As Liz McAuley Clements, wife of Me-262 test pilot Lt. Walter J. "Mac" McAuley Jr., writes, "Youth was the saving grace. Of course, the men probably had moments of excruciating fear, though they would assure their spouses that their own ability far exceeded any pilot's in the outfit." If they felt fear, they never showed it to their wives or fellow pilots as they attempted to live normal lives in base housing at Skyway Park and dined at the 8-Ball on North Main Street in Dayton, where a T-bone steak, french fries, and a drink cost $1.75. By the end of World War II, nearly half had lost their lives. Capt. Jim Fitzgerald and Capt. James Little, both West Point graduates and survivors of prisoner-of-war camps, were killed in routine test flights, while others, like Capt. William C. Glasgow, died when their experimental aircraft failed in spectacular ways.

By 1947, the growth of new suburbs around Wright Field made it difficult to continue test-flying over increasingly populated areas, and the news that former Wright Field test pilot Chuck Yeager had broken the sound barrier meant that supersonic aircraft would soon be arriving. Though Wright-Patterson Air Force Base would continue to manage new aircraft development and acquisition, by 1951 all flight-testing had moved to Muroc Army Air Field (now Edwards Air Force Base) in California.

Many accidents at Wright Field were minor, as demonstrated by the P-40N (s/n 42-1964) pictured above and P-47C-1 (s/n 41-6126) pictured below. Unlike earlier eras in flight-testing when pilots were encouraged to push an aircraft to its limits, during World War II, test pilots at Wright Field were trained to fly an aircraft at an exact speed, altitude, rate of climb, and revolutions per minute and to duplicate their actions repeatedly without variation in order to determine if the aircraft was meeting performance requirements. (Both, AFLCMC.)

On March 14, 1943, Lt. Col. Osmond "Ozzie" Ritland and Col. Nathan "Rosie" Rosengarten were testing the first British de Havilland Mosquito delivered to the AAF when a fire broke out in the port engine, forcing the crew to bail out just west of Dayton. Ritland broke his back on landing and was hospitalized for seven months. Rosengarten survived and became project leader for tests of the German rocket-powered Me-163 Komet and the Air Force's first test engineer of jet-propelled aircraft. He later served as an investigator of UFO sightings and was instrumental in creating Project Blue Book. (AFLCMC.)

In late 1946, a Bell YR-13 helicopter arrived at Wright Field for evaluation. The aircraft was damaged during a hard landing at Patterson Field (Area C) on March 18, 1947, and was returned to Bell for repairs. In 1948, the YR-13 entered service with the US Army as the Bell H-13 Sioux. Long after the Army and the Air Force became separate branches, Wright Field continued to be a test facility for Army helicopters, especially for their rotors. (AFLCMC.)

Pictured flying over Dayton (above), Messerschmitt Me-262 (Werknummer 111711) was captured on March 30, 1945, when its pilot flew it to Frankfurt/Rhein Airport on its maiden flight and surrendered to US forces. The first new Me-262 to be captured, it was shipped to Wright Field where it became the first German jet tested by the Army Air Forces. Displayed at the Wright Field Air Fair in October, 1945, "711" was lost on August 20, 1946, when an engine caught fire during a comparison flight with a Lockheed T-33A. Lt. Walter J. "Mac" McAuley Jr. bailed out, becoming the first American pilot to bail out of a jet. The plane impacted alongside Route 68 two miles south of Xenia, Ohio, creating one of only two Me-262 crash sites (below) in the United States (a second Me-262 crashed on landing at Greater Pittsburgh Airport on August 19, 1945). (Above, NMUSAF; below, AFLCMC.)

Wright Field's "Darkest Day" was Sunday, May 27, 1945, when tragedy struck during the field's last Victory War Bond Air Show. Part of the show was a flyby of three highly decorated combat veterans: Capt. William C. Glasgow (right) flying the experimental Curtiss XP-55 Ascender (below); Maj. Richard "Dick" Bong, the highest-scoring American ace of World War II, in a Lockheed P-38 Lightning; and Capt. Dominic "Don" Gentile in a North American P-51 Mustang. Glasgow, 28, of Niagara Falls, New York, was a P-40 pilot with over 80 combat missions over North Africa. Shot down over Germany, he had escaped a prisoner-of-war camp. Glasgow held the Silver Star, Distinguished Flying Cross, Purple Heart, and Air Medal with six oak leaf clusters. Glasgow's XP-55 (s/n 42-78847) was a rear-engine pusher design with a troubled test history at Wright Field. (Both, Andrew Glasgow.)

Glasgow's XP-55 was supposed to make a low pass from north to south in front of the grandstands while performing a slow roll. As he reached the southern end of the field, the XP-55 failed to recover from its roll and pancaked onto the field, bursting into flames. As 70,000 people watched, the burning wreckage skipped over Airway Road, tearing through 150 feet of fence before crashing into a lot across the street where visitors had parked. Captain Glasgow was killed in the initial impact. Across the street, Ohio highway patrolman Cpl. Charles "Brownie" Brown was directing cars pulling into the lot as the XP-55 suddenly crashed through the fence, engulfed in flames, barely missing Brown and destroying his motorcycle. The worst was yet to come. (Both, Andrew Glasgow.)

Wesley Roehm, 23, had just pulled into the parking lot with his wife, Susan; 20-month-old daughter, Donna Irene; five-week-old daughter, Nina Lee; and Susan's friend Kathleen Eyre, 22, when the XP-55 came crashing through. Kathleen had been holding baby Nina, and threw her out the window as the car was engulfed in flames. Wesley died at the hospital later that day, while Kathleen and Donna died two days later. Susan lived two more weeks, long enough to make arrangement for Wesley's parents to raise Nina, who escaped with only burned hands. Nina Lee Hampton is now a mother and grandmother living in Marysville, Ohio. (Andrew Glasgow.)

The honor guard for Capt. William C. Glasgow's funeral in Niagara Falls, New York, includes Capt. Don Gentile (second from left) and Maj. Dick Bong (third from right). Two months later, Bong would be killed while flying a Lockheed P-80A. Gentile would perish on January 28, 1951, in a Lockheed T-33A. The Curtiss XP-55 crash led to significant changes in air show rules, including prohibiting aerobatics while flying toward spectators. The cause of the crash was never determined, but was likely stability problems inherent to the XP-55's design. (Andrew Glasgow.)

Perhaps the most bizarre accident ever to occur at Wright Field was the loss of a Fairchild C-82A Packet (s/n 44-23014) on July 14, 1949. The aircraft was performing parachute drop tests out of Patterson Field (Area C) when it declared an in-flight emergency. With the right engine on fire and the electrical system down, the pilot was diverted to Wright Field's 6,478-foot southwest-northeast runway. Touching ground three-quarters of the way down the runway, the C-82A ran off the end of the runway and across a wide grassy area before crashing through a fence surrounding the staff parking lot in front of Buildings 14 and 15. (Both, AFLCMC.)

After crashing through the parking lot fence, the C-82A struck over two dozen cars before flipping onto its back. Base fire and crash crews were on the scene in moments, evacuating the crew members and searching the destroyed automobiles for causalities. Fortunately, all the cars were empty, and no one on the ground was injured. The crash would have seemed comical if it were not for the tragic loss of M.Sgt. Lloyd S. Lubitz, who leapt from the plane just before it struck the fence. The rest of the plane's crew survived with only minor injuries. Many local insurance agents received some interesting claims the next day. (Both, AFLCMC.)

The Wright family burial plot is located in Dayton, Ohio, at Woodland Cemetery and Arboretum, Section 101, Lot 2522. The plot is the burial site for Wilbur Wright, Orville Wright, their father, Milton Wright, mother, Susan Catherine Wright, and sister, Katherine Wright Haskill. In 1999, Otis and Ida Wright, twins born in 1870 who died shortly after birth, were removed from Greencastle Cemetery, a small graveyard in southwest Dayton, and reinterred alongside their parents and siblings. Woodland Cemetery is also the resting site for Col. Edward Deeds, Lt. Col. John Henry Patterson, inventor Charles F. Kettering, and humorist and author Erma Bombeck. (AFLCMC.)

In 1948, Wright and Patterson Fields merged as part of the reorganization of bases following the establishment of the US Air Force in 1947. Dedicated on January 13, 1948, the new base was renamed Wright-Patterson Air Force Base. This photograph shows the combined bases as they appeared shortly after the dedication of the new Air Force Museum (Building 489, the long white building at lower center) on September 3, 1971. The triangular runways of Wright Field (Area B) are at bottom, while the massive 10,000-foot B-36 Runway of the former Patterson Field (Area C) is at top. Today, Wright-Patterson Air Force Base encompasses over 1,600 buildings located on 8,176 acres of land. As of 2010, the base had 27,406 military and civilian employees, the largest payroll of any air force base. Wright-Patterson Air Force Base is now the largest aerospace research facility in the world and is at the center of mankind's next great challenge—the exploration of space. From its humble beginnings as Orville and Wilbur's flying field to its role in aircraft testing during World War II to today's role in aerospace research, the base continues to earn the right to bear the name of the inventors of flight. (AFLCMC.)

DISCOVER THOUSANDS OF LOCAL HISTORY BOOKS FEATURING MILLIONS OF VINTAGE IMAGES

Arcadia Publishing, the leading local history publisher in the United States, is committed to making history accessible and meaningful through publishing books that celebrate and preserve the heritage of America's people and places.

Find more books like this at
www.arcadiapublishing.com

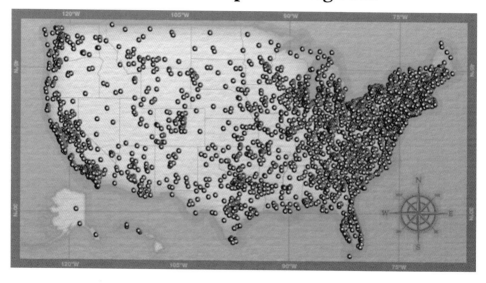

Search for your hometown history, your old stomping grounds, and even your favorite sports team.

Consistent with our mission to preserve history on a local level, this book was printed in South Carolina on American-made paper and manufactured entirely in the United States. Products carrying the accredited Forest Stewardship Council (FSC) label are printed on 100 percent FSC-certified paper.

MADE IN THE